The Persians

An Enthralling Guide to the History of Persia and the Persian Empire

Free limited time bonus

Stop for a moment. We have a free bonus set up for you. The problem is this: we forget 90% of everything that we read after 7 days. Crazy fact, right? Here's the solution: we've created a printable, 1-page pdf summary for this book that you're reading now. All you have to do to get your free pdf summary is to go to the following website:

https://livetolearn.lpages.co/enthrallinghistory/

Once you do, it will be intuitive. Enjoy, and thank you!

We forget 90% of everything that we've read in 7 days...

Get the free printable pdf summary of the book you've read AND much, much more... shhhh...

Enter Your Most Frequently Used Email to Get Started

DOWNLOAD FREE PDF SUMMARY

© Enthralling History

Table of Contents

Introduction

Traditionally known as Persia, the Iranian Plateau boasts a rich and ancient history. In recorded written accounts, it goes as far back as the Assyrian Empire, which began in the late 10th century BCE. However, the history of the region goes back much further to the movements of many nomadic tribes to the Iranian Plateau that established empires in this fertile and strategic land.

The term Persia itself denotes the Indo-European peoples who migrated to the region and created their settlements under Assyrian and later Median rule. Later, this civilization would go on to establish its own dynasty. The Persian Empire refers to the kingdom that spanned over two centuries and is rightly believed to be the largest empire of ancient times.

The history of the Iranian Plateau is divided into three phases, given the extensive and rich succession of civilizations it was home to. The prehistoric period consists of the earliest evidence of civilization in the region, dating back to around 100,000 BCE. The protohistoric period, which started in the 1st millennium BCE, was next. The final period is based on the rule of the Achaemenid Empire, of which extensive written records can be found. This empire spanned from the 6th century to the 4th century BCE.

While the region was home to many different empires over the course of these three periods, the empires did not exist in isolation. In reality, these empires often coexisted and moved through the annals of history in various capacities, sometimes as the subjugated and later as the rulers. Since the region attracted the migration of many nomadic tribes, it consequently came to possess a rich and illustrious history, all of which have contributed to the culture, religion, and languages of the region today.

The recorded history of Iran begins with the Assyrian Empire, which ruled over Mesopotamia and the various ethnic groups found within it until its downfall. History then follows the rise of the Medes, a seemingly unsuspecting nomadic tribe that migrated to Iran and lived in relative peace until they one day rose to rule vast lands. The Median Empire saw a meteoric rise but also fell quickly to make way for the largest empire in ancient history.

This book elaborates on the rise of the Persian Empire and how it managed to expand its domain, covering much of Asia and Africa. As notable as this accomplishment was, this book also explores the downfall of one of the greatest empires to have ever existed. This text discusses the impact of the Persian Empire on the sociocultural landscape of Persia and its continued influence today. The Persian Empire is still remembered, long after its demise, for its art, religion, military, language, and governance.

PART ONE:
PERSIANS AND MEDES

Chapter 1: The Origins of the Medes and the Persians

The beginning of the Iron Age in Iran was marked by a significant cultural and historical change that occurred in the region, which was experienced well before anywhere else in the Near East. While this shift began around 1250 BCE, iron artifacts did not appear in the Iranian Plateau until much later, during the 9th century BCE. Since no true written records existed in the region until the advent of the Assyrian Empire, much of the historical understanding of Iran during this time comes from archaeological excavations.

One of the most notable cultural movements in Iran during this time, as indicated by indirect historical references found among neighboring ancient civilizations, was the migration of the Median and Persian ethnic groups. The Medes and the Persians became the two dominant groups in Iran by the mid-9th century. The Medes occupied more widespread areas, and their importance increased significantly.

The Rise of the Medes

The large groups of migrants moving into Iran during the 2nd millennium are believed to be the ancestors of most modern-day Iranians. While these migrants were initially believed to be Aryans, recent archaeological evidence suggests the Aryans were descended from the tribes that originally migrated to Iran from the north.

Around the 7th century BCE, the Assyrian Empire sought to conquer Iran from the east through to the west and found most of eastern Iran occupied by the Medes as far as modern-day Hamadan. In western Iran, the Medes occupied regions mixed with indigenous non-Iranian people. The Medes had already infiltrated much of the eastern Zagros region and were steadily pushing into the west, reaching the borders of Mesopotamia in some spots.

The movement of the Medes and other Iranian peoples can be traced from the east to the west by the passage provided by the natural mountain topography of the region. The locals resisted the infiltration from this new and growing power and were often assisted by the Assyrians, the Elamites, and the Urartians from northwestern Iran. These powers were only too happy to help contain a growing threat and to further their own interests.

Origin of the Medes

Limited written and archaeological evidence has raised some questions as to the true origin of the Medes. They were an Indo-Aryan people who began moving in from the western end of the Iranian Plateau. One of their earliest mentions was among the Assyrian records in Mesopotamia. The Medes were subjects of the Assyrians until the Assyrian Empire was overthrown by the Medes in the 7th century BCE.

Media is often believed to be the first Iranian kingdom, which eventually took over the various tribes that populated the region, unifying them under a single banner. Much of this perception of the Medes' success came from their geographical position since they were located close to Mesopotamia. They were mentioned in the written records of the Mesopotamians, while other previous kingdoms were not. This suggests that the Medes may not have been the first Iranian kingdom but simply the first one that made it into the chronicles of neighboring empires.

Mythology

One version of where the name Media originates from states it came from the name of the sorceress Medea in Greek mythology. She is the daughter of King Aeëtes of Colchis and the granddaughter of the sun god, Helios. Medea is gifted with prophetic sight and agrees to help Jason, the leader of the Argonauts, to steal the Golden Fleece from her father. In exchange, he has to take Medea with him.

While Medea goes on to marry Jason, she later kills her two sons in a fit of rage to punish Jason when she finds him with another woman. She then escapes to Athens to start a new life. She later leaves Greece after failing to establish her son as king of Athens. The Medes are said to have taken their name from Medea since they deposed the Assyrians, just as Medea deposed the king of Corinth, father to Jason's new bride.

The Persians

The Persians, along with the Medes, had migrated to Persis or modern-day Fars by the 10th century BCE. The Persian dynasty traced its ancestry back to Achaemenes, though there is no historical record of the existence of such a person. The earliest noted reference to the Persians appears in Assyrian records, where they denote a people living in the Sumerian region.

The Persians were composed of five major tribes, the most important one being Pasargadae, of which the Achaemenids were a clan. Following their entry into Iran, the Persians had, by the 1st millennium BCE, established themselves in southwestern Iran. The Persians were conquered by the Assyrians and later the Medes, who overthrew the former to establish their own kingdom. But under the rule of Cyrus the Great, the Persians revolted, overthrowing the Medes to establish the Achaemenid Empire.

Origin of the Persians

Many believe the Persians were horse-riding nomads who peacefully settled in Parsa for some five hundred years. Yet there is little record of how they ended up on the Iranian Plateau. Regardless, by the 7th century BCE, they had taken over Anshan, an Elamite territory, to establish their rule. Their leaders came to be known as kings of Anshan, although they remained subjects to the Assyrians and later the Medes.

The Persians played a role in the final downfall of Assyria. After the overthrow of the Neo-Assyrian Empire in the late 7th century BCE, the Median Empire was concentrated around Media, a region of political power and cultural influence. The Persians remained under the authority of the Medes until their revolt in 552 BCE. After that, the Persians extended their kingdom over the remainder of the Iranian Plateau, also assimilating the indigenous, non-Iranian peoples: the Elamites and the Mannaeans.

Basis in Mythology

The name Persia is believed to originate from Greek mythology with Perseus, the founder of the Perseid dynasty. Mythology paints him as the hero who slew the Gorgon Medusa and founded the city of Mycenae. He is believed to be one of the greatest Greek heroes.

Perseus was a demigod born to Zeus, the god of thunder. He went on to marry Andromeda, daughter of Cepheus and Cassiopeia, rulers of the mythical Aethiopia. Their descendants went on to rule Mycenae, the most powerful city of the Peloponnese. The Persians were believed to be familiar with the story since one of the Achaemenid kings, Xerxes I, tried to leverage it to turn Argos against Greece to aid in the Persian invasion of the region.

The Elamites and the Assyrians: Precursors to the Persians

Before the Medes and the Persians, Iran had played host to two other major dynasties that shaped its history and culture. First came the Elamites, a civilization that spanned thousands of years, from about the 3rd millennium to around the 6th century BCE. As the Elamite civilization began to decline, the Assyrian Empire began to grow, taking power around the 10th century BCE.

The Elamite Civilization

The Elamite civilization occupied the regions of the modern-day Iranian provinces of Ilam and Khuzestan. While the Elamites referred to their land as Haltami, the region is referenced several times in the Bible, referring to both a land and Noah's grandson. There is much debate as to the origin of the Elamites, though most historians believe they were indigenous to the Iranian Plateau.

Not much is known about the civilization since their language does not compare to any others around that time and is yet to be deciphered. Most of the references to the region are found in Akkadian, Assyrian, and Sumerian texts. At times, these texts contradict archaeological evidence, limiting the understanding of the true extent of the Elamite civilization.

Rather than a united region, the Elam civilization was composed of people spread out over a specific region and ruled under the separate leadership of various cities. These included Anshan, Awan, Susa, and Shimashki. Historians divide the civilization into four distinct periods:

- Proto-Elamite Period
- Old Elamite Period
- Middle Elamite Period
- Neo-Elamite Period

Artifacts and archaeological evidence suggest the Elamites had developed expansive trade relations with the subcontinent of India and also traded with Mesopotamia and regions to the east. The Elamite Empire was established by Shutruk-Nakhunte and took shape during the Middle Elamite period. The empire spanned over western Iran and much of Mesopotamia.

The downfall of the Elamites came after their alliance with the Medes in the takeover of the Neo-Assyrian Empire, which helped establish the Median Empire. The Elamite civilization did not disappear entirely until the Sasanian Empire rose up in the 3rd century CE. Until then, the Elamites continued to exist under various empires, although they were no longer rulers themselves.

The Assyrian Civilization

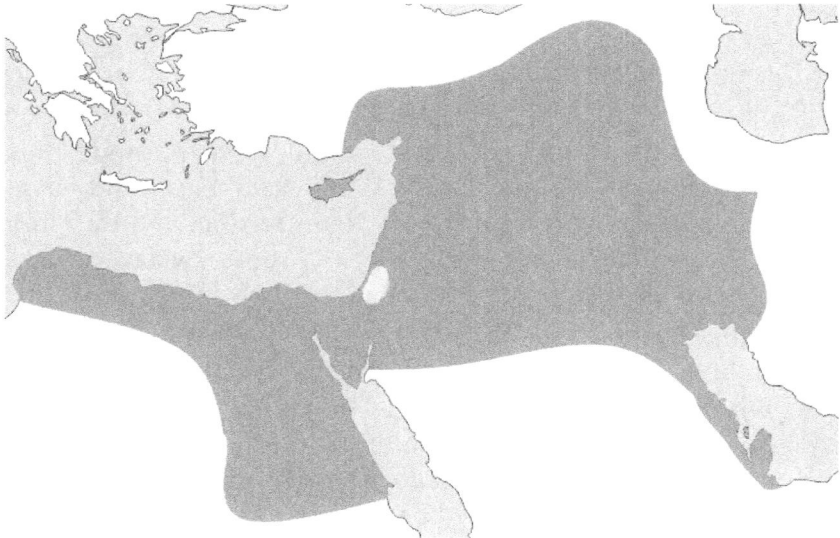

Neo-Assyrian Empire.
Puffoco, CC BY-SA 4.0 <https://creativecommons.org/licenses/by-sa/4.0>, via Wikimedia Commons; https://commons.wikimedia.org/wiki/File:Neo_Assyrian_Empire_671_B.C.gif

The Assyrian Empire occupied regions of modern-day northern Iraq, Asia Minor (modern-day southeastern Turkey), and parts of Egypt between the 10th and the 7th century BCE. The civilization was birthed in the Babylonian city of Ashur, where merchants became wealthy and influential through trade in the Anatolian Peninsula. The name is thought to originally derive from the Mesopotamian god of the same name.

Given the influence of the first ancient kingdom of Mesopotamia, the Assyrians spoke and maintained written records in Akkadian until they adopted Aramaic, which originated in Syria. Being one of the greatest Mesopotamian civilizations, the Assyrian Empire is marked by great economic and military growth. The Assyrian rule is divided by historians into three periods:

- The Old Kingdom
- The Middle Empire
- The Late Empire or the Neo-Assyrian Empire

The Old Kingdom began with the city of Ashur, which had existed since the 3rd millennium BCE and was occupied by nomadic people. The date of the city's official formation is associated with the building of the temple of Ashur by Erishum I around 1900 BCE. It was an important commercial center, especially the port of Kanesh, which proved to be highly lucrative for the city. The port was home to much commercial activity, with merchants setting up and managing extensive businesses.

With the wealth earned through this trade and the trade relations established with Anatolia, Assyria was able to gain power and influence. Trade with Anatolia introduced the Assyrians to iron, and they went on to perfect ironworking, forging weapons like swords, javelins, and spears, which helped them achieve military superiority.

During the Middle Empire, Assyria temporarily fell under Mitanni rule. The Mitannis rose up around the 15th century BCE. After the Mitanni kingdom was taken over by the Hittites, the Assyrian king, Eriba-Adad I, gained influence in the Hittite court. The Assyrians saw an opportunity. They began planning to spread their kingdom outside of Ashur to areas previously occupied by the Mitanni.

Assyrian King Adad-nirari I, who defeated the vassal King Shattuara I of Mitanni and expanded Assyrian control, instated a deportation policy to prevent future uprisings. It was carefully devised to prevent inhumane treatment but was intended to drive the local population out of the region to be replaced with Assyrians. Deportees were carefully matched to a specific region based on their skills and where they would be most useful. Families were never separated.

This kind of leniency did not last in the Neo-Assyrian Empire. The empire underwent ruthless expansion. While the Assyrians used decisive military tactics, most notably siege warfare, they did not mistreat their prisoners. All were treated as citizens, regardless of if they were born Assyrian or acquired through conquest.

The Medes and the Persians

The Persians ultimately established their empire and developed one of the most influential and successful dynasties in the Middle East. The Persian takeover of the Medes united the people of Iran under one rule. Before this, the Persians had existed in disparate groups, hailing from different regions and past empires and leading nomadic lifestyles.

The Persians and the Medes had existed independently, though their movements in Iran overlapped for much of history. Both people groups brought their own distinct cultures, traditions, and languages to the Iranian Plateau, and both held great influence over the region. While there is a lack of written sources prior to the Achaemenid Empire, making it difficult to map the true extent of the Median Empire, the available evidence suggests both civilizations contributed to the culture and growth of the Iranian Plateau. However, the power, influence, and identity of the Medes dissolved under the unifying banner of Persia.

Chapter 2: From Deioces to Astyages: The Median Empire

Northeastern Iran, present-day Iraq, and south and eastern Anatolia fell under the rule of the Median Empire. The lack of recovered records has made it difficult to discover much about the empire, and what little is known is based on the records of neighboring dynasties, such as the Mesopotamians. The Medes were believed to speak a language that most closely resembled Old Persian. Polytheism is believed to have been practiced, although it had Zoroastrian influences.

The empire is often credited with having been created by Deioces, who was able to unite various tribes in the region in the 7th century BCE. He is also believed to have founded its capital city, Ecbatana, which became the center of the Median kingdom. However, other historians believe it was his grandson, Cyaxares, who gathered together the Median tribes and defeated the Assyrians once and for all. While the empire was eventually overthrown by the Persians, it left a lasting legacy behind, which is still the subject of study and debate.

Overview of the Median Empire

The 1st millennium BCE saw the movement of nomadic cattle herders from central Asia to the Iranian Plateau. They spoke an unspecified Aryan language and infiltrated the northern side along the Zagros, settling among the locals. The Assyrian King Shalmaneser III first mentions the existence of such people in his kingdom, although they were perceived as hostile outsiders.

In truth, the Medes existed in scattered tribes, reaching from the Zagros to the edge of Mount Damavand. Since they were perceived as the enemy, Assyrian tribal leaders launched attacks against the Medes, managing to subdue many of them. However, they could not conquer all of the Median tribes, and historians believe this series of Assyrian attacks united the different Median tribes and ultimately resulted in the fall of Assyria.

The nomadic lifestyle of the Medes, which led them to the Iranian Plateau in the first place, shifted to permanent residence for another reason. The region occupied by the Medians offered direct access to trade routes with Babylonia.

Since Media controlled the east-west route, it gained many economic benefits. The Medians made trade one of their main occupations, along with agriculture, and began to gain influence in the region. It also led to the rise of Ecbatana as an important trade center.

In terms of agriculture, the Medes found immensely fertile land in the Zagros region. Its valleys and plains were well known for producing high-quality clover. The fruitful lands could support a wide variety of cattle, sheep, goats, and horses, as well as large populations. The Medes were located in an economically strategic region, which aided their subsequent rule of northern Iran.

The Median Tribes

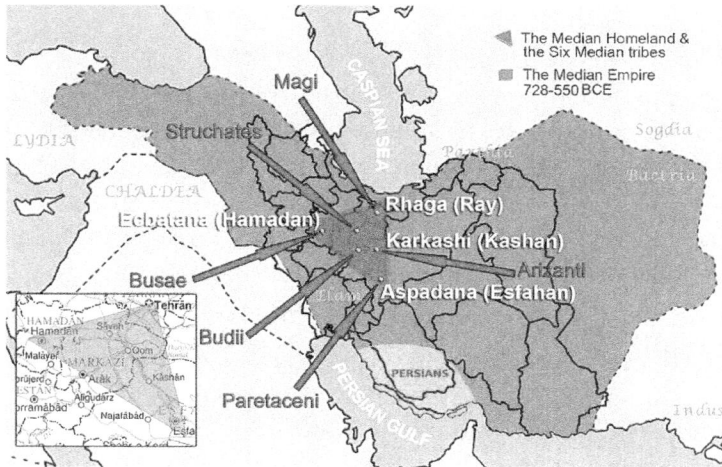

Media Proper

Key Mirza, CC BY-SA 4.0 <https://creativecommons.org/licenses/by-sa/4.0>, via Wikimedia Commons; https://commons.wikimedia.org/wiki/File:Median_Empire_Map_2222.jpg

The Median civilization is believed to have consisted of six tribes, which were later unified as a single nation and ruled by Deioces. All six tribes resided in what was known as Media Proper, a triangular region that fell between Ecbatana, Aspadana, and Rhagae. Beyond their geographical location, little is known about the tribes besides some basic information.

The Busae tribe could be found in and near the capital of Ecbatana, close to what is today known as Hamadan. The Struchates tribe could also be found in Ecbatana. The Paretaceni tribe was found in and near Aspadana, which is today known as Isfahan.

The Arizanti tribe could be found in the province of Kashan, as well as on its outskirts. The Magi tribe resided in Rhagae, which is modern-day Tehran. Of the six tribes, only the Magi were known to be comprised of a sacred caste who looked out for the spiritual needs of the people.

The Median Language and Religion

The Medians are believed to have spoken an Old Persian language called Median. However, no written texts have been discovered in the Median language. Some later records do show examples of Median literature, as well as discoveries that some believe are written clauses on which Deioces based his rule. While the Median language itself has not been discovered, words of Median origin are found in Old Persian languages.

Regarding their religion, the Medians were paganistic. However, Zoroastrianism, a henotheistic religion (one main god with the possibility of the existence of other lesser deities), has its roots during this time. The Magi tribe was believed to provide spiritual advice to the Medians. They are believed to have practiced traditions common with the Zoroastrian religion, and as such, they are seen as being linked to this religion. By the 6th century, Zoroastrianism had begun spreading in western Iran.

The Rise and Fall of the Median Empire

The Median Empire is believed to have lasted around 130 years. During that time, four kings are believed to have ruled. However, there is conflicting evidence as to the identity of these kings and the duration of their rule. Regardless, historians have identified and estimated each of the four kings and their period of rule as the following:

- Deioces, 7th century BCE
- Phraortes, mid-7th century BCE (twenty-two years)
- Cyaxares, late 7th century BCE to early 6th century BCE (forty years)
- Astyages, early 6th century BCE to mid-6th century BCE (thirty-five years)

The Rule of Deioces

Deioces is credited with uniting the Medes, but it would be more accurate to say that the Medes united and then elected him as their leader. He was a renowned judge and regarded as just and infallible. As the Medes began to rebel against Assyrian incursions, Deioces took the opportunity to try and establish a justice system in his own village.

This undertaking soon spread to other Median villages, and he was often sought after to help resolve local issues. Overwhelmed with the fame he had accumulated as a judge and arbiter, he resigned. In response, the Medians chose to appoint him as their king, and he went on to rule for approximately fifty-three years.

Deioces appointed guards for his protection and set about constructing the Median capital, which was enclosed in seven concentric circles. Ecbatana was intended to be the uniting point for the Medes within Media Proper. Within the city, Deioces also built a fortified castle, from where he could manage the affairs of the empire. Deioces's brand of law and order involved appointing "watchers" and "listeners," which is similar to the term "the king's eyes and ears."

By establishing his own kingdom, Deioces became the first Median king to gain independence from the Assyrians. However, his activities also drew the attention of the Assyrian king, Sargon II. Deioces became a more prominent threat to Sargon when he offered his allegiance to the Urartian king, Rusa I, against the Mannaeans, who were Assyrian allies. His previous participation in an unsuccessful rebellion against the Mannaeans sealed his fate. Sargon entered Media, captured Deioces, and exiled him to modern-day Syria.

Deioces's Legacy: Phraortes

The second king of the Median Empire originally held the position of village chief of Kar Kashi. During his reign, he is believed to have continued fighting wars against the Assyrians, although he remained unsuccessful in overthrowing that empire. Phraortes developed an alliance with the Cimmerians, an eastern Iranian nomadic tribe, against the Assyrians.

During his twenty-two-year rule, Phraortes is believed to have conquered the Persians and other smaller Asian tribes of the time. However, little is actually known about his rule due to unreliable accounts and limited evidence. His subjugations came under the direction of the Assyrian Empire until he broke the temporary alliance and waged battle against them. The Assyrians took the offensive, and Phraortes was killed on the battlefield. The Assyrians then took over the lands he had conquered as part of their own empire.

The Legacy Continues: Cyaxares

Phraortes was succeeded by his son Cyaxares around 625 BCE. He allied with the Babylonians and took up the fight against the Assyrians, laying siege to their capital city, Nineveh, in Upper Mesopotamia.

The siege lasted three months before the invading army was able to break through the city's defenses. The city fell quickly, and it was burned and plundered by the Medes and the Babylonians. The Assyrian king, Sin-shar-ishkun, was killed in the battle, and Ashur-uballit II, possibly Sin-shar-ishkun's son, took the throne.

It is believed that the fall of Nineveh dealt a major blow to the Assyrian Empire. Over the following three years, the Neo-Assyrian Empire struggled but ultimately fell to the Medes and the Babylonians. In the decades to follow, the Assyrian Empire disappeared almost entirely.

Cyaxares was a successful military leader and launched campaigns against the Assyrians and Scythians. He focused on military efficiency, reorganizing the army based on the designations of bowmen, spearmen, and cavalry. He also instituted distinct uniforms.

During his forty-year rule, he subjugated the Kingdom of Mannaea, and the Urartians, the latter of which lived in what is today Armenia.

After the fall of Nineveh and Nimrud, the Medo-Babylonian alliance took over Assyrian lands, which were divided between the two to rule. The Medes took Harran, which became the Assyrian capital after the fall of Nineveh. Thus, Cyaxares was the one who ultimately defeated the Assyrians and established the Median Empire as a force to be reckoned with.

The Fall of the Scythians

The Scythians were an eastern Iranian people who migrated from central Asia to the Pontic Steppe. Their skill in mounted warfare gave them dominance over the Cimmerians in the region, allowing them to cross the Caucasus Mountains. This led to the Scythians frequently invading West Asia. After invading the Near East, they settled in the Mannaea region in northwestern Iran.

Initially, the Scythians used their martial skills to work as mercenaries, meeting much success in the Near East and Asia Minor. The Scythians also led an army against the Assyrians in Mannaea in the early 7th century BCE but were eventually defeated.

After losing Mannaea, the Scythians launched a series of attacks against the Assyrians, reaching as far as Egypt, which had been under Assyrian rule. The king of Egypt at the time, Psamtik I, bribed the invaders to retreat into Syria. At the same time, the Assyrians were facing a crisis in the form of civil wars and the Medo-Babylonian campaign.

The Assyrians forged an alliance with the Scythians, who helped them during the siege on Nineveh. This led to a battle between the Medes and the Scythians, which resulted in defeat for the Medians. This defeat led Cyaxares to seek revenge, and he invited a large number of Scythians to a banquet. There, they were inebriated and then murdered by the Medes.

The Last King of Media: Astyages

Astyages, son of Cyaxares, was the last of the Median kings. Before his death, Cyaxares had been fighting a five-year war with the Lydian Kingdom in western Anatolia. The Battle of Halys (also known as the Battle of the Eclipse) ended the war in favor of the Medes just before Astyages's succession to the throne. As a result, he inherited a vast empire, which included many Assyrian lands.

Existing accounts of Astyages's rule paint conflicting pictures, with some portraying him as cruel and others as a benevolent leader. A common belief, which many believe to be a myth, is that Cyrus the Great was the grandson of Astyages through his daughter. Astyages tried to kill Cyrus while he was still an infant based on a dream that indicated his downfall at the hands of Cyrus. However, there is no solid evidence of this ever occurring.

Astyages met his defeat at the hands of Cyrus the Great, who led a war against him around the mid-6th century BCE. The Medes fought back, ultimately leading to the siege and plunder of Ecbatana. Astyages was taken prisoner, and the fall of the empire's capital marked its end. The once-great Median Empire fell under Persian rule.

The Median Empire's Legacy

The Median Empire did not last long. Compared to the Persian Empire that followed, the Median Empire was a blip in Iranian history. However, the contributions made by the empire to the history, culture, and religion of the region cannot be underestimated. The fall of the Assyrian Empire at the hands of the Medes changed the course of Iran and paved the way for the next great empire.

The limited written evidence regarding the Median Empire makes it difficult to get a detailed idea of the events that occurred during its rule. What little is known about the empire based on recovered archaeological evidence and writing from neighboring civilizations shows that the Median monarchy experienced a successful rule. Its economy and military flourished. Just before its fall, it had amassed a large geographical area. But this region now fell under Persian rule.

PART TWO:
THE PERSIANS – RISE AND PEAK

Chapter 3: Cyrus the Great

The Achaemenid dynasty was one of the most powerful empires in the world. The success of Cyrus II (better known as Cyrus the Great) can be seen in the Persian Empire's military and geographical expansion. The Achaemenid Empire grew to be the largest of its time, extending from Anatolia to the subcontinent of India and central Asia.

Cyrus the Great is also credited with introducing many innovative practices in his kingdom. While a popular myth believes Cyrus was descended from Astyages, as the grandson who was destined to overthrow the Median Empire, historical sources suggest he was descended from Teispes, the son of Achaemenes, who is credited as the founder of the Achaemenid clan.

The development of the Persian Empire began with the conquests of Cyrus the Great. While it continued to grow and advance after his rule, Cyrus's leadership created the foundation of the ancient world's largest empire.

The Early Life of Cyrus the Great

Cyrus the Great.
DiegoColle, CC BY-SA 4.0 <https://creativecommons.org/licenses/by-sa/4.0>, via Wikimedia Commons; https://commons.wikimedia.org/wiki/File:Cyrus_the_Great_of_Persia.jpg

Cyrus the Great was born to Cambyses I in the 6th century BCE. Before him, his father, grandfather (Cyrus I), and great-grandfather (Teispes) all held the throne in Anshan. Cyrus would later marry Cassandane, the daughter of Pharnaspes, who bore him two sons, Cambyses II and Bardiya, and three daughters, Atossa, Artystone, and Roxane. After the death of his wife, Cyrus declared public mourning, which lasted for six days.

Although many scholars believe that Cyrus was not related to Astyages, it is still a popular belief and is worth taking a look at. According to legend, Astyages had a dream about his grandson growing up to overthrow his kingdom and kill him. Fearful that this might come true, he ordered the assassination of his grandson, which ultimately failed. Instead of killing Cyrus, the infant was given to a shepherd family.

When Astyages discovered that Cyrus was still alive when the boy was ten years old, he decided against killing him. Cyrus was returned to his true family and apparently spent much time in Astyages's court. If the legend is to be believed, Astyages's dream ultimately came to be true since Cyrus grew up to overthrow the Median Empire. The truth of Cyrus's ancestry is still much debated, and it is likely that the tale of Astyages attempting to kill Cyrus in infancy is only legend.

The Rise of Cyrus II

When Cyrus became king of the Achaemenids in the mid-6th century, the throne was a vassal of the Median king, Astyages. It is unclear as to what ultimately led to the conflict between the Medians and the Persians, who still observed allegiance to the Medes. Regardless, Astyages sent an army, under the command of his general Harpagus, to attack Cyrus.

However, Harpagus held some enmity against Astyages. Instead of attacking Cyrus, he encouraged him to revolt. He defected to the Persians, bringing half the army under his command with him. The Persian revolt is believed to have lasted for around three years. It ended in the capture of the Median capital city, Ecbatana.

The Battle of Hyrba

The Battle of Hyrba was the first encounter between the Persians and the Medians. It was during this battle that Harpagus turned on Astyages. According to legend, Harpagus told Cyrus about the battle ahead of time, giving him time to prepare.

Cyrus allegedly wrote to his father, asking him to prepare the cavalry and infantry. He took these men to Hyrba, where they destroyed the Medians. Astyages realized he was no longer dealing with a revolt and sought to invade and destroy the Persians. Cyrus had proven himself and began expanding his empire.

Battle of the Persian Border

Following the Battle of Hyrba, the Persians moved to the Persian border to protect it against the Medians. Astyages marched to the border and engaged the Persians in combat.

This battle wasn't as intense or exciting as the one at Hyrba. It lasted for two days and saw Cambyses fight alongside his son. Although the Persians proved themselves, it wasn't a very convincing win. Even so, it was clear the Medians were outmatched.

It is unclear how many battles the Medians and the Persians fought, although it is believed the fighting lasted for three years. In the end, Cyrus emerged victorious when he captured the capital, Ecbatana. He also captured Astyages and brought him back to his homeland in Persia, where he remained until his death. Following this victory, Cyrus built the city of Pasargadae, which was to serve as the capital. The city consisted of several monumental buildings, two palaces, and the tombs of Cyrus and Cambyses II.

Major Conquests under Cyrus the Great

Cyrus was able to conquer two other major empires besides the Medes: the Anatolian Kingdom of Lydia and the Babylonian Empire in Mesopotamia. Under Cyrus's rule, the kingdoms of the Near East were united as a single nation, creating the largest empire of its time. His son, Cambyses II, was later able to acquire regions of northeastern Africa.

The skill and efficiency with which Cyrus expanded his kingdom speak to his capability as a ruler and military leader. He laid the foundation for an empire that lasted over two centuries.

Conquest of Lydia

Before the ascension of the Medes, Lydia had been an ally to the Assyrians. During the Median campaign against Assyria, the Medes forged an alliance with the Cimmerians. The Lydian Kingdom had suffered from constant Cimmerian invasions, so the Medes-Cimmerian alliance did not help matters, and the two nations remained at war during Median rule. When the Persians conquered the Medes, Lydians took notice of the rising power. Their king, Croesus, had doubts about Cyrus's rise to power.

Following a divine message from the Greek Oracle of Delphi, Croesus decided to lead a campaign against the Persians. He launched a surprise attack on the Persians across the Halys River in the mid-6th century, believing he was fated to destroy the rising empire. The Battle of Pteria led to an inconclusive result, with the Lydian army retreating toward their homeland.

In a strategic move, Cyrus pursued the Lydians, hoping to launch a surprise attack in their capital city of Sardis. The two armies met at Thymbrara. Although the Lydians were caught off-guard, they still heavily outnumbered the Persians. The ensuing Battle of Thymbrara marked the last confrontation between the Persians and the Lydians. Given the disadvantage of numbers, Cyrus resorted to a tactical approach. During the battle, the Persians placed their baggage camels, which were mounted by cavalrymen, at the forefront. The stench of the camels repelled the Lydians' horses, disrupting their charge.

The Persians successfully fought and laid a fourteen-day siege on Sardis, where the Lydians had retreated. The city eventually fell, and the Persians conquered Lydia, bringing its over six centuries of independence to an end.

Instead of destroying the newly conquered nation, Cyrus maintained his tolerant approach. Local cultures, laws, religions, and traditions were allowed to continue, and Croesus was admitted into Cyrus's court. Cyrus's accepting approach helped the Persian ruler attain the loyalty of the Lydian people.

The Fall of Babylon

The fall of Babylon is marked by the Battle of Opis, which took place around 539 BCE. Not much is known about the specific events of the battle, which was the final encounter between the Persians and the Babylonians. Written sources regarding this final standoff refer to Cyrus fighting the army of Akkad, which refers to the Babylonian Empire. But who the army was led by is not known and never appears to have been recorded. However, the popular belief is that the son of Babylonian King Nabonidus, Belshazzar, led the final assault against the Persians.

Little is known about the Babylonian army or its military capabilities. However, it is believed the Babylonians suffered a quick and sudden defeat. It may be that the Babylonians were unprepared for the onslaught levied by the Persians.

Babylonia was already suffering in the geopolitical sphere around the time of the Battle of Opis. It was surrounded by the Persians to the east and west and the Phoenicians to the north, making it more vulnerable to attack and at risk of being trapped. Severe social and economic problems within the Babylonian Empire had already taken root and were wreaking havoc. The region suffered plague and famine, and the unorthodox religious approach of their king had already turned the Babylonians against him. Cyrus used this unrest and turmoil in the region to his advantage. Cyrus is believed to have struck a deal with a Babylonian provincial governor to defect to the Persians, which brought the region of Gutium under Cyrus's control. Gutium was a strategically significant frontier that enabled a strong Persian offensive.

The battle led to a decisive Babylonian defeat. Following their victory, the Persians plundered and looted. Some historical sources suggest that massacres were carried out against the Babylonians; however, the basis and accuracy of such a belief are not set in stone.

Shortly thereafter, the Babylonian city of Sippar is said to have surrendered to the Persians, who marched on Babylon without further resistance. Babylonia was the last great power in West Asia not yet under Persian rule. Cyrus the Great was later declared king of Babylonia, bringing its independence to an end.

In 530 BCE, Cyrus the Great led a campaign into central Asia against the Massagetae. He was killed, although the sources differ on how. Most believe he died while fighting, although some believe he was killed by Tomyris, the queen of the Massagetae.

Regardless of how he died, Cyrus left a vast and successful empire to his son, Cambyses II, although his rule was short-lived and less successful than his father's.

The Persian Legacy: Cyrus the Great

Cyrus the Great is remembered as a leader with many achievements, the greatest of which is the empire he amassed within a span of just thirty years. He took over three great dynasties and brought them under the unified rule of the Persian Empire. During that time, he also gained a reputation as a benevolent and just ruler, examples of which are still cited today.

The Persian Empire's growth was unprecedented, bringing Persian culture into the global sphere. The rise and spread of Persian literature, philosophy, and religion were driven by the empire's growth and the geographical spread of its people. Cyrus's achievements form a very noticeable part of ancient history that continues to have a great impact on modern times.

As a ruler, Cyrus the Great was known by many titles, such as the Great, the Elder, the King of Kings, and the King of the Four Corners of the World, which all speak to his character as a ruler and conqueror. He was known for his exceptionally tolerant approach to different peoples, as he allowed the practice of local religions and cultures in any land he conquered. His system of governance was one that honored freedom, independence, and civil rights, rejecting any notion that rulers of his time needed to adopt a vicious, autocratic approach. Cyrus's military aptitude is exemplified by the size of his empire, which stretched from the Mediterranean Sea to the Indus River.

The Persian Empire went on to build the largest road network of its time. With the Royal Road, the Persians were able to establish trade connections across the Middle East. This road network, combined with the legacy of diplomacy and tolerance that Cyrus the Great left behind, marked the success of the empire.

Cyrus the Great is also referenced in the Bible. He appears as a liberator, as the Messiah who freed the Jews from Babylonian captivity.

Needless to say, Cyrus the Great's influence can be seen in his leadership style and in the success of the empire he built.

Chapter 4: Cambyses II and the Fall of Egypt

Following the death of Cyrus II in 530 BCE, his son took on the mantle of king. Cambyses II inherited what was, at the time, the largest empire to ever exist. Still, he continued in his father's footsteps and carried on campaigns to expand the empire. While many of his crusades were successful, Cambyses II did not possess his father's knack for strategy and planning, so he ended up losing some previously conquered lands.

Before his father's death, Cambyses II had already taken on many royal duties. During New Year festivals, he is known to have acted as king in his father's stead. Cambyses was largely responsible for managing Babylonian affairs and was appointed regent while Cyrus campaigned in the east. He officially served as vice-king of Babylonia until his ascension to the throne.

Cambyses II

Cambyses II.
https://commons.wikimedia.org/wiki/File:Cambyses_II_capturing_Psamtik_III.png

Cambyses II was the firstborn of Cyrus and Cassandane, making him heir to the throne. Historical reports suggest Cambyses had a younger brother, Bardiya (also known as Smerdis), with whom he had a rivalry when Cambyses became king. This same rivalry reportedly led to the death of the second king of the Achaemenid dynasty.

After the conquest of Babylon, Cambyses was appointed the crown prince of the region and later acted became vice-king. The Cyrus Cylinder, which is an important piece of evidence that talks about aspects of Cyrus's rule, also mentions Cambyses as being blessed by Marduk, the Babylonian patron god. Due to Cambyses's early involvement with Babylonian affairs, he was often referred to as the king of Babylonia long before he actually held the title.

Historical records differ on the subject of Cambyses's marriage. Some suggest he married Phaedymia, daughter of Otanes, the latter of whom is believed to be the brother of Cassandane. Other sources suggest that he may have married his two blood sisters, Atossa and Roxane. Such types of incestuous relationships were an accepted part of Zoroastrianism, so this possibly could have occurred. However, there is no definitive proof to suggest such a marriage ever existed.

Some reports also exist of Cambyses II being a "mad king." These mostly come from the accounts of Herodotus, a Greek historian who recorded the Greco-Persian Wars in great detail. While Herodotus offered many examples he believed indicated Cambyses's madness—such as his alleged marriage to his sisters—there is little other evidence supporting this. Such views are believed to be the product of oral tradition passed on among the Egyptians. Regardless, Cambyses is believed to have faced his fair share of problems during his rule as the king of the Achaemenid Empire.

Persia under Cambyses II

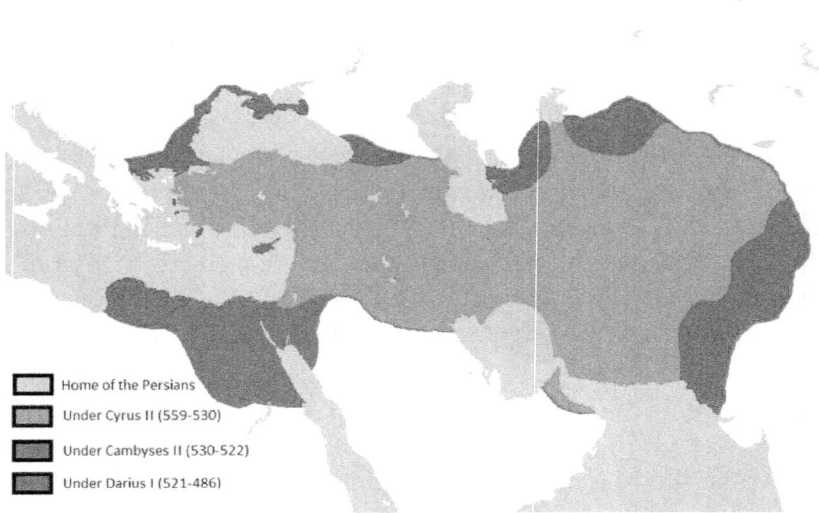

The Persian Empire.

Since Cyrus had already appointed his eldest son as regent before his death, Cambyses was able to take the Persian throne without trouble. More specifically, Cambyses was given the title of king of Babylon and king of the lands, and he carried out these duties on behalf of his father until Cyrus's death. There is little to report of the early years of Cambyses's rule, as they remained rather uneventful. A short two-year famine in Babylon in that period did raise some concerns. Many believed that it was an indication of the god's disapproval of the new king.

The first event of notice that Cambyses was a part of as regent king was his inauguration as the king of Babylonia during the New Year ceremony. This celebration signified the divine approval for the new king and was an important tradition in Babylonian culture. Since Cyrus had created a reputation of religious tolerance and acceptance within his empire, Cambyses's participation was crucial. However, little is known about the exact details of the rituals and customs involved in the ceremony.

What little is known is based largely on Herodotus's account and indicates the people's disapproval of the new king. Cambyses apparently showed up for the ceremony in the wrong clothing and was surrounded by armed guards. Babylonian tradition forbade the presence of arms during the procession and is believed to have earned him the displeasure of the priests present at the ceremony.

Cambyses eventually stepped away from his ruling duties in Babylonia. It is unclear what the reasons for the resignation were, but many believe the events of the New Year celebration may have contributed, at least in part. It could have happened because of his other commitments as king of Persia. Whatever the reason, this move led to speculation regarding Cambyses's ability to serve as king of the Achaemenid Empire.

Whether he was successful as king or not is a matter of perspective. His most notable achievement was the conquest of Egypt, a campaign that had been planned by Cyrus. However, Cambyses's rule over Egypt is surrounded by controversy and claims of him being unfit for the role.

Conquest of Egypt

Since the conquest of Egypt had been planned by Cyrus the Great, it is likely that he would have ventured into Africa following his failed campaign against the Massagetae. Since Cyrus died in battle there, Cambyses took on what would be the most important and significant conquest of his reign. Egypt was conquered in 525 BCE, five years after Cambyses became king.

The attack on Egypt was not a surprise, and the Egyptians were prepared to meet the Persian army. The Egyptians had forged an alliance with the Samians from the Greek island of Samos, who were able to provide naval support. This would have helped launch an attack along the route they were to take to reach Egypt. They also enlisted the help of mercenaries from Greece and Caria.

The Case of Egypt

The defeat of Egypt at the hands of the Persians came as a result of a strategic and effective move by Cambyses II. A particularly revered aspect of ancient Egyptian culture was the worship of cats. They were associated with the goddess Bastet, who often appears in Egyptian art as a woman who possesses the head of a cat.

Bastet was worshiped as the goddess of domesticity, childbirth, fertility, and cats. She acted as protection for households from diseases and evil spirits, particularly those that might affect the children and women of the house. As a venerated goddess, offending her would result in severe punishment.

Harming cats was one of the ways the goddess Bastet could be offended. Cats were sacred to the ancient Egyptians, so hurting one was a punishable offense. Killing a cat would result in a death sentence for the offender. And Egypt's defeat by the Persians came about because of their high regard for cats. Cambyses II knew the role cats played in their culture and used it to his advantage to conquer Egypt.

The Battle of Pelusium

Historical accounts of what transpired before the conquest of Egypt suggest that Pharoah Amasis II of Egypt offended Cambyses II, which led to the war. However, it is believed Cambyses had already been preparing for a campaign since it was something his father had planned to do before he passed. The Persian king had reportedly asked for Amasis's daughter's hand in marriage. Rather than refusing, Amasis reportedly sent his predecessor's daughter to Persia. Nitetis, the daughter who was sent, was also offended since it was against Egyptian custom to give away women to foreign rulers. She was adorned in clothes and gold and presented to Cambyses as Amasis's daughter.

When Cambyses discovered the deception, he accused Amasis of sending him the wrong wife and sought to get retribution for the insult. Preparations were made to launch a Persian assault. However, while many sources do suggest that Amasis had done something to earn the Persian king's wrath, they do not all support the story of a fake wife.

Whatever the reason may have been, it seems an attack on Egypt by Persia was inevitable. The Persian Empire had undergone rapid growth under Cyrus's leadership, and Cyrus was eyeing the region before his death. The Assyrian conquest of Egypt also left the impression of Egypt being a land that could be easily acquired. Egypt had been ill-equipped to take a stand against the Assyrian assault, so it did not seem likely that it could do any better against Persia's superior forces.

When the two armies met at Pelusium, the Egyptians were able to withstand the attack. Their help from Greece was undoubtedly of great assistance since the allied force was able to prevent the Persians from advancing farther. But Cambyses used his knowledge of the Egyptian religion to secure his victory. He ordered the image of Bastet to be painted on his soldiers' shields and had cats, dogs, sheep, and other animals sacred to the Egyptians lead the army into battle.

This move compelled the Egyptians to lay down their arms since they did not wish to shoot at either the image of their goddess or risk harming the animals. Those who did not surrender fled to seek refuge in Memphis. The Persians killed many on the battlefield of Pelusium that day and chased the others, with Memphis falling after a relatively short siege. Thus, Egypt came under Persian rule. Psamtik III, the son of the pharaoh, had led the charge. He was taken prisoner but was reportedly treated well until he attempted to revolt against the Persians.

The Conquest of Libya

The Persian conquest of Libya was more a matter of alliance. The king of Cyrene, a city in eastern Libya, likely did not want to go to war with a force like the Persian army, and he forged an alliance with the Persians following their conquest of Egypt. When the king was killed during unrest in the region, the Cyrene queen, Pheretima, extended an invitation to the Persians to enter the region, intending to avoid further fighting and hostilities. The Persian expedition into Libya ran for close to a year, resulting in the conquest of Libya.

The Persians were able to infiltrate as far west as modern-day Benghazi. A king loyal to the Persians was installed, and Cyrenaica became a Libyan region under Persian control. It remained so until the Egyptian rebellion and the defeat of the Achaemenid dynasty by Alexander the Great.

The Libyans of Cyrene and Barca in northeastern Libya did not resist Persian entry; in fact, they willingly accepted Cambyses's authority. They also sent him offerings as a show of submission and acceptance of his rule. To return the favor, Cambyses sent the widow of the Egyptian pharaoh back to Cyrene.

According to other historical accounts, Cambyses was unsuccessful in his campaigns in Ammon, east of the Jordan River, and Ethiopia. Some sources suggest the reason for the loss was Cambyses's failure to lead his men. According to Herodotus's accounts, Cambyses ordered his men to march to Ethiopia without sufficient provisions. However, this account is not supported by any other evidence, and it appears more likely that the challenges of the campaign, including the long distance, may have caused Cambyses to withdraw.

The Lost Army

The legend of the Lost Army is one of the great enigmas surrounding Cambyses II. Historical accounts narrate an army of some fifty thousand men who marched to Ammon to attack the oracle who would not legitimize Cambyses's rule of Egypt. This army is last reported to have reached the "Island of the Blessed," though it is not known where this was located. The next report is of a sandstorm that blew over the troops, burying them forever. That was the last this army was seen or heard from.

Since then, many historians and explorers have attempted to recover archaeological evidence proving the existence and the subsequent loss of this army. No definitive proof has been found, although the discovery of human bones in 2009 in the Sahara Desert raised speculation that they may belong to the lost army of Cambyses.

The Madness of Cambyses

While the conquest of Egypt was considered Cambyses's greatest achievement, some historical sources cite him as an unfit ruler. His actions as pharaoh mark him as unstable. The historian Herodotus said he was mad. Whether such accounts are true cannot be said for certain, but they certainly paint a picture of Cambyses II as a man who did not deserve the responsibilities and duties of a kingdom as vast as the Persian Empire.

There are many faults attributed to Cambyses during his reign as pharaoh of Egypt. While he kept with tradition and took on the titles of "King of Upper and Lower Egypt" and "descendant of Ra, Horus, and Osiris," he is believed to have gone too far. Some sources report that he engaged in extensive propaganda to portray himself as the rightful ruler of Egypt and to show the legitimacy of his ascension to the throne. Reportedly, he attempted to portray himself as having Egyptian heritage. He had himself crowned in the temple of Neith, the goddess who created the universe, as a religious ritual and even made sacrifices to the gods.

Cambyses is reported to have engaged in numerous examples of brutality during his rule over Egypt. Some sources claim he looted temples, scorned the local religion and gods, and did not hesitate to defile royal tombs and other places of religious significance. Many of these reports come from Herodotus; there are no other sources or recovered archaeological evidence that supports these claims about the

Persian king.

Cambyses was also accused of killing a bull sacred to the Egyptians, Apis. The bull was believed to be the physical manifestation of the god Ptah and was therefore revered by the Egyptians. According to Herodotus, Cambyses ordered the killing of Apis, which directly opposed his father's approach to religious tolerance. As with the other accusations, there is no evidence to be found in other sources or reported accounts of Cambyses's rule to support this claim. The closest evidence is Cambyses's order to have an Apis buried in a sarcophagus, yet there are no reports of an order to kill one.

Finally, Cambyses was also accused of killing his brother, Bardiya. Bardiya had a claim to the throne. According to some reports, Cambyses was worried Bardiya might contest his ascension to the throne and chose to deal with this potential threat by having it eliminated. There are also many other outlandish claims, such as Cambyses assassinating the son of one of his courtiers. He may have ordered the premature burial of twelve Persian nobles and the execution of several courtiers. Such examples are used to justify the claim that Cambyses was out of his mind and unfit to serve as ruler.

The Fall and Legacy of Cambyses II

Other than his conquest of Egypt, Cambyses II could not hold any great achievements to his name. While he was initially believed to have been blessed by the gods when he became king, this notion was later questioned as his rule progressed. In many ways, he was seen as a man who failed to fill the shoes of his father.

Others hold a different view of his leadership and credit him for introducing many improvements to the Persian army. He did manage to expand the Persian Empire, most notably with the conquest of Egypt, and the Persian military came to be known as one of the best of its time.

Cambyses II likely died from a wound to the thigh that became infected. He died in Syria in 522 BCE. His rule was relatively short and did not end on the best of terms. Following his death, a rather bloody succession crisis began, which would mark the future progress and later decline of the Persian Empire.

Chapter 5: Darius I: Looking Westward

Darius I eventually succeeded Cambyses II as the new king of Persia. His initial rule was punctuated by revolts and rebellions, which were spurred by the events that led to his rule. During this time, the Persian Empire expanded to the east into the Indian subcontinent and to the west, including Thrace-Macedonia in the Balkans and the Caucasus. The empire's growth brought increased wealth and power to the Persian king. However, it also brought him greater challenges, with Darius rarely stumbling upon a moment of relief due to a seemingly unending series of wars and revolts.

Early Life

Darius I was part of the Achaemenid nobility. He was the son of Hystaspes, who was a provincial governor, or satrap, of Bactria and Persis. Although Darius played a role in the Persian Empire before his rule, he had no legitimate hereditary claim to the throne. Based on historical records, he was a spearman during the Persian conquest of Egypt, and his father had been an officer in Cyrus's army. Darius held a special role in Cambyses II's army, serving as his spear carrier, and was tied to the royal family by marriage.

Darius was married to two of Cyrus's daughters, Atossa and Artystone, with whom he had six sons. Atossa gave birth to Xerxes, who would go on to succeed Darius as the ruler of Persia. Darius was also reportedly married to Parmys, the daughter of Bardiya, who bore him one son. He is also believed to have married two other noble women, with whom he had several children.

A popular story of unverified origin states that while Cyrus was on his final campaign, he saw a dream that he believed showed Darius taking over his kingdom. He had already installed Cambyses as regent, so Cyrus suspected Darius of treason. He ordered Hystaspes to return to Persis and watch over Darius until his return. Any plans Cyrus had regarding Darius never came to light since he perished during the campaign.

Becoming King

Reported accounts from Darius I and historians narrate variations of the circumstances under which Darius came to the throne. The common thread that follows these accounts is the assassination of Bardiya, the younger son of Cyrus the Great, at the hands of his brother, Cambyses II. Reportedly, Cambyses did so to suppress any idea of a fight for the throne, which he believed he had a right to.

Bardiya's death was not well known, and a usurper by the name of Guamata was believed to have taken the throne pretending to be Bardiya. During a revolt that broke out among the Iranian people, Guamata, as Bardiya, was installed as the new king. Darius and six other nobles killed Guamata, and Darius took the throne for himself in 522 BCE.

Darius the Deceiver

The Darius Seal.
Osama Shukir Muhammed Amin FRCP(Glasg), CC BY-SA 4.0
<https://creativecommons.org/licenses/by-sa/4.0>, via Wikimedia Commons;
https://commons.wikimedia.org/wiki/File:The_Darius_seal._Darius_stands_in_a_royal_chariot_b
elow_Ahura_Mazda_and_shoots_arrows_at_a_rampant_lion._From_Thebes,_Egypt._6th-
5th_century_BCE._British_Museum.jpg

Since Darius was accompanied by six nobles on his mission to depose the fake king, it is unclear how he was chosen to take the throne. Sources, which are not wholly verified, report that the seven men discussed the future of the kingdom. Some wanted to establish a democracy, while others wanted an oligarchy. Darius wished to continue the monarchy and convinced the others that a republic would lead to corruption in the region.

Reportedly, six of the seven men decided on a test that would determine who the next monarch would be, with one of the men abstaining. The test required the men to mount their horses outside the palace. The man whose horse was the first to neigh with the rising sun would become king. It is believed that Darius I did not wish to leave his rule to chance and engaged in trickery to ensure his horse would be the first to neigh.

Darius's plan was carried out by his slave, who put the scent of a mare favored by Darius's horse on his hand. As the sun rose, he allowed the horse to sniff his hand. Darius's horse caught the mare's scent and neighed. As fate would have it, lightning and thunder followed the horse's call, and the other men immediately knelt before Darius, accepting him as monarch. The thunder and lightning were largely interpreted as divine acceptance, and Darius was believed to have been chosen by the gods to rule Persia.

Other accounts suggest this report of Darius's rise to power may be false. It is believed by some to be a fabrication created by Darius to legitimize his murder of Bardiya and his own ascension to the throne. It is true that Darius attempted to gain further support for his rule by claiming to be descended from Achaemenes, the ancestor of Cyrus the Great, who is credited with founding the Achaemenid dynasty. In truth, Darius had no relation to Achaemenes and did not belong to the same family as Cyrus.

The New Monarchy Begins

The beginning of Darius's rule was not smooth. While the six noblemen may have accepted him as the king of Persia and blessed by divine will, the rest of the kingdom did not. Whether the man Darius killed was a usurper or the son of Cyrus did not matter. That man was believed to be Bardiya, so Darius, therefore, was believed to be the killer of the rightful king of Persia.

Darius found himself facing revolts across the Persian Empire that were propelled by his assassination of "Bardiya." The eastern provinces, in particular, including Media and Babylonia, saw widespread disruptions, with men claiming to be the true Bardiya and setting up independent governments. These were not coordinated uprisings; they were scattered rebellions headed by different individuals and motivated by various purposes.

The dispersed rebellions were no march for Darius's army, which suppressed and defeated at least nine rebel leaders. By 519 BCE, he had put an end to most of the uprisings. In the following year, he visited Egypt, which he had declared to be a rebel state for the insubordination of its satrap, Aryandes. The satrap was sentenced to death, and Darius was, at last, able to establish his authority as the king of the Persian Empire.

Expanding the Empire: Indus Valley Conquest

The Persian Empire's conquest of the Indus Valley began with Cyrus the Great, who invaded the regions west of the Indus River. The Achaemenid Empire was able to expand its control to regions of modern-day Pakistan, and the Indus Valley campaign continued from the 6th century to the 4th century BCE. India's trade relations with the Near East are believed to have placed it in the sights of the Achaemenid dynasty. Starting in 535 BCE, Cyrus the Great is believed to have conquered regions as far as the Indus River. Other sources suggest he may have conquered regions up to Gandhara, located in northwest Pakistan.

Persian records of the campaign show that Darius I may have crossed the Himalayas around 518 BCE and progressed as far as the Jhelum River. Persian inscriptions during Darius's reign refer to the expansion of Persian rule to a region called Hindus, which is believed to refer to the Indus Valley. Sources suggest this conquest was not intended to expand the Persian Empire. Frequent invasions from the north led Darius to seek secure regions for his wealth and holdings in the east. The promise of untold riches, including gold, ivory, peacocks, and apes, piqued his interest in what lay in the Indus Valley.

Darius is believed to have commissioned an expedition along the Indus River to discover regions and trade routes. The expedition began in the north, with his men traveling around the Iranian coast, and ended in Egypt. Based on reports, the Persian king occupied an unspecified region near Gandhara and established the Indian Ocean as a trade route along the coast of Iran. The Behistun Inscription, which was erected by Darius near Kermanshah in Iran, states that the regions of Gandhara and Hindus were part of his empire.

Again, what specific region Darius was referring to as Hindus remains disputed. Most historians agree it must have been somewhere along the Indus River since there is some evidence of Persian presence. Most believe the region of Hindus may include the modern-day province of Sindh in Pakistan, while a few hold the belief that Darius may have proceeded northeast of Gandhara, though there is little evidence to support the latter claim.

The Persians are believed to have built many forts along the Indus River, at least one of which housed the Persian governor in Hindus. The reported wealth of the region was true, as it is believed to have made massive contributions to the Persian treasury in gold and other precious metals.

Persian influence in the Indus Valley had the effect of establishing better communication channels between the regions beyond those of trade relations. The organized administration the Persians brought with them impacted the region's management greatly. Stamped coins were introduced in the valley, and the Persians are also believed to have brought the Aramaic language and texts with them into the region.

In return, Indian concepts of mysticism, religion, and reincarnation were introduced to Western thought. The influence of such teachings and beliefs can be found in the works of Near Eastern and Greek philosophers of the time. The most notable contribution of the Indus Valley remains its treasures. It is also believed Darius I brought back an Egyptian canal into use that may have served as a predecessor to the modern Suez Canal.

The Scythian War

The Scythian War was a campaign led by Darius I against the Scythians, an Iranian-speaking nomadic tribe. The Scythians had previously invaded Media during the rule of Deioces and been defeated yet remained a constant nuisance to the Persian Empire. Their revolt during the rule of Darius threatened the trade between central Asia and the regions near the Black Sea, as these areas were held by the Scythians.

Because the Scythians led a nomadic lifestyle, they were able to avoid a direct confrontation with the Persian army. The Persians, on the other hand, had been suffering significant losses from Scythian invasions, as the Scythians destroyed food in the regions they entered and poisoned the wells, the first recorded use of scorched-earth tactics.

Darius had a bridge of boats constructed to cross the Black Sea, conquering regions of eastern Europe on his way to the Scythians. His invasion of Scythia was frustrating, as the Scythians evaded the army and moved eastward, destroying the countryside behind them. They blocked wells, destroyed pastures, and only engaged in small scuffles with the Persian army but generally maintained a distance when retreating, causing the Persians to chase after them.

While the Scythians' tactics helped them evade a direct confrontation, bringing the Persians deeper into unfamiliar lands, it also led to the loss of many Scythian lands. The Persians moved deep into modern-day Ukraine with no lands to capture and no army to fight. Regardless, Darius still held the upper hand, as his army was able to survive off of cultivated Scythian lands. Meanwhile, the Scythians laid waste to much of their lands, damaging them and their allies in the process.

A month into the campaign, Darius halted at Oarus, an unidentified Scythian river, where he built eight forts as a frontline defense. His army was suffering from fatigue, limited supplies, and rampant sickness. Darius failed to bring the Scythians into a direct confrontation but managed to take over or destroy most of their lands. The Scythians, for their part, were not bested by the Persians but had lost significant territories to them. The campaign concluded with a stalemate, though it is reported the Scythians developed a newfound respect for the Persian army. Fearing a lost cause, Darius abandoned the Scythian chase and turned his armies toward Thrace.

Conquest of Thrace and Macedonia

After turning away from Scythia, Darius diverted his attention toward Thrace. Under the leadership of his general Megabyzus, the Persian army headed east. Thrace was known as a populous region, and following a successful campaign around 514 BCE, Megabyzus set up establishing Persian rule in the region. This included removing many of the Thracian tribes from the region and transporting them back to Persia, which was meant to weaken the locals in case of an uprising and for them to serve as slaves in Persia.

After Thrace, Megabyzus turned his attention to Macedonia. The Macedonian campaign did not involve force. The Persians demanded that the Macedonian king surrender to the authority of Darius I. Megabyzus demanded a tribute made by earth and water. The Macedonians initially surrendered peacefully, becoming a vassal state to Persia. After the Ionian Revolt, Macedonia helped assert Persian authority in the Balkans.

Suppressing the Ionian Revolt

The conquest of the Greeks by the Persians began with an attempt to conquer Naxos, a Greek island, which ultimately failed. The Persians had already begun to occupy Greek regions following their unfruitful pursuit of the Scythians. At the beginning of the 5th century BCE, Aristagoras, the leader of Miletus, urged the Persian satrap, Artaphernes, to invade Naxos. With Darius's blessing, his cousin Megabates was named leader of the Persian army. A reported quarrel between Megabates and Aristagoras at the pivotal moment before the campaign led to the latter betraying the Persians.

Aristagoras did not want to lose his position as the leader of Miletus, so he encouraged the Ionian states to revolt. The Ionians, along with troops from Athens and Eretria, captured and burned Sardis in 498 BCE. As they made the return march to Ionia, they were followed by Persian forces. A confrontation led to the Battle of Ephesus, where the Ionians were defeated. In 497 BCE, the Persians launched a triple attack, attempting to capture regions lost to the rebellion. The resulting battles did not produce any conclusive wins for either side.

Seeking to put an end to the revolt, the Persian army set out to attack the heart of the rebellion at Miletus in 494 BCE. The Ionians tried to defeat the Persians with their naval force but lost to them during the Battle of Lade. Miletus was besieged by the Persians and captured. After the defection of the Samians, the Ionian revolt ended. The rebellion officially concluded with a peace treaty, which required Ionia to pay tribute to the Persians.

Battle of Marathon

Although the rebelling states had been brought back into the Persian fold, Darius decided that Eretria and Athens needed to be punished for their involvement in the revolt. Darius sent an army to deal with these two city-states. Eretria was sacked, and then the Persians moved to Marathon, a city about twenty miles northeast of Athens.

The Battle of Marathon took place in 490 BCE. The Athenians were aided by a small Plataean force, while the Spartans refused to send aid, citing the ongoing religious festival as the reason for refusal. The Athenian force was able to block the two exits from the city and chose a mountainous terrain for the battle. The unfamiliar and uneven territory made it difficult for the Persian cavalry and infantry to launch a joint attack.

While the Athenians prepared for war, they were outnumbered by the advancing Persians ten times. This battle required the use of wit over force, so the Greeks strategized a direct and sudden attack on the Persians. As the opposing army approached at a casual pace, the Greeks, under the leadership of Athenian general Miltiades, broke into a sudden sprint, forcing immediate hand-to-hand combat.

After a few hours of fighting, the Greeks were able to break through the Persian ranks. Records show the Persians lost some six thousand men that day compared to only about two hundred fallen Greek soldiers. The Persian army fell, and the Greeks celebrated by using the marble blocks the Persians had brought to celebrate their victory to build a monument in memory of their fallen soldiers. Darius I took the defeat as a personal insult and vowed revenge; however, he died before he could bring his plans to fruition.

Succession and Legacy

Darius had been preparing to lead a war against the Greeks when a revolt broke out in Egypt. The heavy taxation in the region, coupled with the forced migration of Egyptian craftsmen, led to rising unrest against Persian rule. This diverted Darius's attention from the Greek campaign and worsened his already failing health. Darius I died soon after, in 486 BCE. His body was embalmed and placed in the tomb he had prepared for himself at Naqsh-e Rostam.

Darius the Great's reign is considered one of the most important periods of the Persian Empire. As the Persian Empire expanded, the reforms introduced by the king improved the living conditions of the people. The laws that were introduced during this time laid the basis for the current laws of Iran.

Chapter 6: Xerxes I: The Persian Empire at Its Peak

When Xerxes inherited the throne, he also inherited a revolt by the Persian satrapy, including the satraps in Egypt and Babylon. The Persians were angry and humiliated by their defeat at the hands of the Greeks. Thus, Xerxes faced a huge responsibility from the outset. While the Persian Empire still held its might, things began to change following the death of Darius I.

Xerxes's most notable effort during his reign remains his campaign against the Greeks. However, it did not solidify the Persian Empire's rule there; instead, it dealt a heavy blow and brought the leadership of Xerxes I into question.

The Life of Xerxes I

Xerxes I was the son of Darius the Great and succeeded his father to the Persian throne. While the legitimacy of Darius's ascendence to the throne was in question, Xerxes was born to Atossa, Cyrus's daughter, and, therefore, came from the house of the rightful Persian dynasty. By historical accounts, Xerxes was raised every bit as the son of Darius and the grandson of Cyrus until he took the throne.

Persian princes are believed to have been raised by eunuchs until the age of seven. They were first taught riding and hunting and later began their education at the hands of aristocratic teachers. Since Zoroastrianism was the major religion practiced in the Persian Empire at the time, Xerxes was taught it. He also served in the Persian military, achieving honors and medals.

Most Persian princes of the time are believed to have been raised in a similar fashion. A note of contention remains on the question of their ability to read and write since the Persians preferred the spoken word over written history. Xerxes maintained his main residence in Babylon until the passing of Darius I.

Accession to the Throne

Before the revolt in Egypt, Darius I had been preparing to lead another expedition into Greece. He had already appointed his son, Xerxes I, as regent, although Darius was never able to set out for Greece before his death. Xerxes believed himself to be the rightful heir to the throne. However, he faced some opposition from his half-brother, Artobazan.

Artobazan was Darius's eldest son; thus, he believed he had the right to the crown. It is believed that Darius chose Xerxes as his successor due to the special privilege he enjoyed, being born to Atossa and being the grandson of Cyrus the Great. Xerxes was also born after Darius had become emperor of Persia, which elevated Xerxes's status as the son of a king. On the other hand, Artobazan was born while Darius was still a commoner.

Xerxes also received the support of Spartan king Demaratis of the Eurypontid line, who was in exile in Persia at the time. This support, along with the authority Atossa and the descendants of Cyrus the Great enjoyed, helped Xerxes take the crown without much opposition in 486 BCE.

The Egyptian Revolt

Xerxes's first concern as king was the rebellion in Egypt, which had pushed his father to his deathbed. It is believed the revolt reached as far as the city of Thebes in Upper Egypt, though not all Egyptians may have supported the Persian opposition. Little else is known about the nature of the rebellion, how far it spread, and what exact measures Xerxes took to deal with it.

However, the general consensus is that the new Persian king marched to the region with his army, suppressing the rebellion. Based on limited accounts, he instated a more severe system of slavery in the region and appointed his brother, Achaemenes II, as the satrap.

Invasion of Greece

After restoring peace to the empire, Xerxes was ready to take on Greece and seek vengeance for his father. Xerxes undertook one of the biggest campaigns in the history of the Achaemenid dynasty.

The preparations for the invasion of Greece are reported to have taken between three to four years. Troops from every satrap were called, and great naval efforts were also made. The resulting military force is believed to be the largest ever seen in the region at that time. Xerxes took the campaign seriously and left nothing to chance.

Battle of Thermopylae

Xerxes's march on Greece led to the Battle of Thermopylae, which was fought at the same time as the Battle of Artemisium. While Xerxes gathered his forces to produce a mighty military, the Greeks did not sit idle. The Greek alliance between the various city-states was led by Athens and Sparta. The Spartan king Leonidas led the army at Thermopylae. The Greeks planned to block the Persian advance in Thermopylae while simultaneously blocking them at sea in the Straits of Artemisium.

In 480 BCE, a Greek army comprising about seven thousand men marched under Leonidas to Thermopylae to block the pass. The Persian army vastly outnumbered the Greeks and was estimated to comprise between 70,000 to 300,000 men. The Greeks were able to hold off the far superior advancing army for seven days. As the battle progressed, the Greeks were able to block the only road leading through the pass.

The Greeks may have endured longer were it not for the actions of a local resident who showed the Persians another pass that ran behind the Greek lines. Leonidas realized defeat was imminent and told most of the army to leave. He remained behind, along with some Spartans, Thebans, Thespians, and helots. Around two thousand Greeks were left behind. They did not surrender to the Persians and fought to their deaths.

The Persian army had foiled the Greek plan to hold off the approach at Thermopylae. While the Greeks suffered defeat, the defense of their home is still cited today as an example of the benefits of training, equipment, and tactical strategies.

Battle of Artemisium

The Greeks planned to block the Persians on land at Thermopylae and their naval force at Artemisium. The Greek allies were able to gather about 271 triremes to await the Persians at Artemisium under the leadership of Themistocles. Before the Persians even reached the Greeks, they were caught in a gale near Magnesia, losing about a third of their fleet. After reaching Artemisium, the Persians again attempted a strategic move and tried to maneuver around the Greeks from the coast of Euboea. They were caught in another storm, and about a third of their ships were destroyed.

For two days, the battle continued, with small skirmishes and engagements taking place. While this resulted in equal losses on both sides, the much smaller Greek fleet could not afford the losses. These skirmishes led to no decisive victory. Once the news of the Greek defeat at Thermopylae reached Artemisium, the Greeks realized their stand at the strait was pointless since it was supposed to be a combined attack.

The Greeks decided to retreat to Salamis, allowing the Persians to take over Artemisium. The Persians also entered Phocis, Boeotia, and Attica. They were even able to take Athens, which had already been evacuated. The Persians then headed to Salamis, seeking a definitive victory over the Greeks.

Battle of Salamis

After the Persians' takeover of Athens, Xerxes was unsure of his next steps. He consulted a war council, the majority of which recommended that he chase after the Greeks in Salamis and come back with a decisive victory. Only Artemisia I of Caria, a Greek ally to the Persians, recommended that Xerxes wait for the Greeks' supplies to run out and then secure a peaceful victory. Xerxes chose to go with the majority opinion and marched to Salamis.

The naval battle that followed in September 480 BCE proved to be a decisive victory—for the Greeks. When the much larger Persian army moved into the Straits of Salamis, their large size became a disadvantage. The Persian fleet struggled to maneuver and organize itself, thus falling into chaos. Seizing the opportunity, the Greeks, led by Themistocles, launched an offensive.

The Persians were defeated, and Xerxes chose to return to Persia. However, he left his military commander Mardonius behind to continue the Greek campaign. Mardonius would go on to lead the Persians in a confrontation at Plataea. By the time Xerxes I returned home, he was humiliated and defeated, and little was left of his army. They were greatly reduced due to a shortage of supplies on their return journey and rampant illness among the ranks.

Battle of Plataea

In 479 BCE, the Persian army led by Mardonius met the Greeks for a final confrontation at Plataea. While the Persians held control of Thessaly, Phocis, Attica, Athens, Boeotia, and Euboea due to their victories at Thermopylae and Artemisium, their defeat at Salamis prevented them from taking over the Peloponnese, which would have connected the Persians to the central part of Greece. This time, the offensive was launched by the Greeks.

The Greek army marched out of the Peloponnese, forcing the Persians to retreat to Boeotia and fortify themselves near Plataea. The Greeks realized a further incursion into Persian-led territory would result in losses, so they refused to move forward, avoiding a direct confrontation for eleven days. As they gathered to retreat due to supply shortages, Mardonius saw an opportunity to attack.

However, the Persian general had misread the situation, as the Greeks were not fully retreating; rather than allowing the Persians to chase them, the Greeks halted and fought the Persians. The resulting battle brought about the defeat of the ill-prepared Persian army and the death of Mardonius. The Greeks trapped the Persians in their camps and slaughtered most of them. The Persians also suffered a naval defeat simultaneously with this land conflict.

Battle of Mycale

The Battle of Mycale in 479 BCE decisively ended the second Persian invasion in favor of the Greeks. The confrontation took place off the coast of Ionia along the slopes of Mount Mycale. As the Greeks mounted an attack on the Persians at Plataea, a fleet set sail to Samos, an island opposite Ionia. The Persians are believed to have encamped at the foot of Mount Mycale, hoping to avoid battle.

The Greeks decided to attack the fortified Persian camps. The Persian army could not withstand the attack and retreated to their camps. However, the Ionian members of the Persian army defected, leading to the Persians' defeat. Their camp was attacked, the Persians were slaughtered, and their ships were captured and burned. The huge losses sustained by the Persian navy and army suppressed the Persians, ending their invasion.

What followed the Persian defeat was the beginning of the Greek offensive against the Persians. In the larger Greco-Persian Wars, their victory against Xerxes's armies was a decisive factor that sealed Persia's fate. For Xerxes, it was a questionable facet of his rule since he lost his army and the people's respect in this humiliating defeat to Greece.

Battle of the Eurymedon

Between the years 469 to 466 BCE, the Persians began to gather forces to lead an attack against the Greeks. The combined army and naval force headed toward the Eurymedon. It is believed the force intended to move through Asia Minor, capturing cities along the way. The Persian plan was to obtain more naval bases and recapture areas that had been lost to the Greeks.

The news of Persian scheming reached the Greeks, who gathered around two hundred triremes to block off the Persian advance. Before the Persians could gather themselves, the Greeks attacked near the Eurymedon River. Many of the Persian sailors abandoned their ships and fled to land.

Greek naval and land forces attacked simultaneously, destroying the Persian camp and over two hundred Persian triremes. The Greeks were also able to take many prisoners. This decisive double victory prevented any further action on the part of the Persians until Artaxerxes's rule.

Xerxes after Greece

Historical reports suggest that Xerxes took the Persian failure in Greece hard. He withdrew, retiring to Persepolis. Any wealth he may have built up through excessive taxation schemes was rapidly depleted by extravagant construction plans. In Persepolis alone, he ordered the construction of a palace called Apadana, a treasury called the Hall of a Hundred Columns, and the Tripylon, or the "triple gate," which connected the palace and the treasury.

Few historical accounts note much about Xerxes I's reign following his defeat at the hands of the Greeks. He is reported to have removed himself from political affairs, retreating into his harem and remaining unbothered by matters of the state. His defeat, as well as his lack of involvement in the empire, has made him perhaps the most notorious ruler of the Achaemenid dynasty.

The King Assassinated

Xerxes I's unpopularity may have contributed to his untimely and violent death. He met his end in 465 BCE when he was assassinated, along with his son Darius II, by Artabanus. It is believed he was a powerful figure in the Persian court and was likely the commander of the royal bodyguard.

After Xerxes's assassination, his son, Artaxerxes I, sought revenge. He killed Artabanus and claimed the throne. The violent end to Xerxes's rule and a similar beginning to Artaxerxes's regime presented a slew of problems in the empire. The people of Persia had already been struggling under Xerxes I, and the change in emperors did not help matters. Widespread revolts broke out across the empire.

Chapter 7: Artaxerxes I and the Egyptian Revolt

Artaxerxes I's reign began in much the same way as that of his father. His succession to the throne was punctuated by violence. Egypt and Bactria, in particular, saw new revolts against Persian rule, and Artaxerxes was forced into clashes within his own regime to reestablish peace.

The rule of Xerxes I had been notorious, to say the least, and his reputation did not help his son. Artaxerxes remained involved in similar conflicts as his father. However, he showcased better military strategizing and ability and made use of cunning tactics rather than force against his enemies.

Artaxerxes I Becomes King

Artaxerxes I.

Artaxerxes was reportedly raised by Artabanus, who was the commander of the king's guard. When Artaxerxes sought revenge for his father's assassination at the hands of Artabanus, he killed the culprit and his sons, the former in a hand-to-hand confrontation. After doing so, he became Emperor Artaxerxes I of Persia in 465 BCE.

Reigning a divisive Persia was no easy task, and these new hostilities added to the unrest within the empire. Another concerning revolt broke out in Egypt, presenting a considerable challenge to the new king. Before his death, Xerxes I had been planning another incursion into Greece, which did not come to fruition before his assassination. Artaxerxes I took on that new responsibility when he inherited the throne.

Artaxerxes I was often referred to as Longhand, reportedly due to a longer right hand. He was married to Damaspia, who gave birth to his son and heir, Darius II. Not much is known about Damaspia, but some reports suggest she may have died on the same day as Artaxerxes.

The Greek Problem

The second Persian invasion of Greece did not end much better than the first and left Persia at a considerable disadvantage. Following the Battle of Mycale, the Greeks took the offensive, continuing the Greco-Persian Wars. The Delian League, which was headed by Athens, continued attacking Persian-occupied regions in the Aegean, even after the Persian forces had withdrawn following their defeat at Mycale.

The Greek incursion Xerxes I had been planning before his death did not end well. He gathered forces to march against the Greeks to put an end to Greek hostilities. This led to the ill-fated Battle of the Eurymedon.

Themistocles Arrives

One of the defeats the Persians suffered in Greece under Xerxes I was dealt at the hands of the Greek general Themistocles. Therefore, it may have come as a surprise when he turned up in Artaxerxes's court. Themistocles had earned disfavor in Greece due to his general arrogance toward the Spartans and his demand to refortify Athens. He was ostracized and later made to stand trial on the charge of treason. He fled, making his way from Argos to Asia Minor, where he presented himself to Artaxerxes.

Artaxerxes accepted his offer of service and his help in defeating the Greeks. Historical records and recovered artifacts, including minted coins, show the Persian king made him satrap of at least three cities and also helped him smuggle his wife and children out of Athens. Themistocles's inside knowledge of Greek activities helped Artaxerxes plan his next move against the Greeks.

Manipulating Sparta

Much tension was caused in Greece due to the activities of the Delian League. It was led by Athens and had banded together for the express purpose of dealing with the Persian threat. The Delian League managed to stop the Persian invasion, and Athens grew powerful and wealthy by exploiting the other members, essentially creating an Athenian Empire. This caused strife with the Spartans, who wanted to be the dominant Greek power.

Artaxerxes used the increasing tensions in Greece to add fuel to the fire. He secretly funded the build-up of Sparta's military while offering gifts, symbolizing peace, to Athens. He then simply allowed the naturally festering unrest to take its course.

Soon enough, the Spartans and the Athenians clashed. Reportedly, the Spartans insulted the Athenians when the latter arrived to help deal with a helot rebellion. Sparta had been growing tired of what it saw as Athenian arrogance and aggression. When the Peloponnesian War broke out, Artaxerxes looked to Themistocles to help him destroy the Greeks.

Accounts vary as to what happened next. Some report that Themistocles had a change of heart at the last minute and was unable to betray his Greek brothers to the Persians, choosing to poison himself instead of helping Artaxerxes. Other accounts suggest Themistocles simply passed away from a natural death before the Persian king could call on him for aid. The Peloponnesian War caused both Athens and Sparta to seek an alliance with Persia; however, no treaty could be reached before Artaxerxes's death.

The Egyptians Revolt—Again

The Egyptian rebellion in 460 BCE came as a surprise for the Persians. Perhaps because Artaxerxes's attention had been focused on the Greeks, he did not foresee the unrest before an outright attack occurred. It was incited by Inaros II, a Libyan prince with connections to the Saite dynasty in Egypt. Inaros discovered the Athenians were planning to attack the Persians in Cyprus and forged an alliance.

The exact date of the rebellion is hard to pinpoint, as different sources suggest a slightly different timeline. However, some reports do suggest that Inaros may have already incited the rebellion before offering an alliance to the Athenians as they prepared to attack Cyprus. Some reports go as far as to suggest that the Persians were already struggling against Inaros's forces and had been pushed into a corner in Memphis by the time Athenian reinforcements arrived.

Regardless, it is agreed the rebels were able to deal heavy blows to the Persians. The Persian satrap of Egypt was killed during the Battle of Papremis, and the Athenian forces were able to take control of the Nile. They then laid siege to Memphis, taking control of most of the region with the exception of the citadels, where Persian soldiers had sought shelter.

The resulting conflict continued for six years, and Inaros, who was supported by the Athenians, proved to be a formidable force. The Persian army was led by Megabyzus, while Arsames, the satrap of Egypt, led the naval force. In 454 BCE, Megabyzus was able to defeat Inaros, just as Arsames defeated the Athenian fleet supporting the Egyptian revolt.

The Athenians made a final effort at the Battle of Prosopitis, which was surrounded by the Nile. The Athenians expected to be able to attack the Persians as their fleet passed by on the Nile. Instead, Megabyzus diverted the delta, leaving a dry and barren land behind, which his army used to march past the Athenian vessels that were now useless. Most of the Athenians died because of injuries, the harsh weather, and the lack of supplies. With the rebellion suppressed, the Persians were able to reestablish their rule and restore peace in the region.

Megabyzus Revolts

When Megabyzus brought forth captives from the rebellion, including Inaros II, Amestris, the queen-mother and wife of Xerxes, ordered their beheading. Megabyzus pleaded against this, as he had assured the prisoners they would not be harmed and that their lives would be spared. Artaxerxes initially chose to honor Megabyzus's word until he was pressured by his mother to have the prisoners executed.

Megabyzus saw this as a betrayal and revolted. He defeated the Persian generals sent against him in single hand-to-hand combat, not wanting to create a civil war in Persia. Finally, Amestris herself arrived as part of an embassy to make an offer of apology and restore peace.

Believing his honor to be reinstated, Megabyzus accepted, ending his revolt.

Peace of Callias

Following the suppression of the Egyptian rebellion, Athens decided to continue with its initial planned attack on Cyprus while still fighting the Peloponnesian War with Sparta. Around 450 BCE, the Athenians gathered a large fleet from member states of the Delian League and charged Cyprus, which they found heavily fortified by Megabyzus's army.

Despite seeing an unbreachable island before them, Cimon, the leader of the fleet, still chose to attack. He was killed during the ensuing confrontation, and the remaining Athenians withdrew from Cyprus. Artaxerxes did not want any more interference from Athens, so he sent an embassy with a truce proposal. The Peace of Callias was negotiated, bringing an end to the hostilities initiated during the reign of Darius I. The Peace of Callias was enforced for about ten years and was broken by Athens in 439 BCE when it attacked Samos.

Artaxerxes in the Bible

Artaxerxes I giving his letter to Ezra.
From The New York Public Library https://digitalcollections.nypl.org/items/510d47e4-134f-a3d9-e040-e00a18064a99

Various historical accounts all report Artaxerxes to be a kind-hearted and gentle ruler. He is discussed in the Books of Ezra and Nehemiah. His treatment of the Jews granted them and other people of the Persian Empire a great deal of freedom and autonomy.

Ezra is believed to be a priest who was sent to Jerusalem by Artaxerxes to standardize the Law of Moses. He then went on to rework the Mosaic Law, which would revamp the lives of Jews in Jerusalem. Nehemiah, on the other hand, is thought to have been a member of Artaxerxes's court, where he served as a cupbearer. One day, the king saw him upset and asked him to state his issue. Nehemiah had been worried about Jerusalem's walls, which lay in ruins and left the city defenseless. He hoped for support in the restoration effort.

During Cyrus the Great's reign, Babylon was liberated, and the Jews, who had been held there by the Babylonians, were finally able to return home to Israel. Cyrus had also decreed that the Jews be offered lavish gifts as they left their Persian homes. The Jews who returned to Israel began to work on rebuilding their temple and walls; however, they continued to face opposition from surrounding lands.

Some of the people who objected to the return of the Jews wrote Artaxerxes, levying false accusations against the Jews and claiming that they refused to pay taxes. Based on this information, Artaxerxes ordered the rebuilding of the wall be ceased, allowing the opposers to march to Jerusalem to prevent the Jews from continuing construction. However, Artaxerxes continued Cyrus's policy of tolerance. Once he realized the true situation, he allowed Ezra to head to Jerusalem. Ezra was assured that the Jews would have as much silver, gold, and other amenities as they needed. Artaxerxes also removed tax obligations from those serving in the temple.

Artaxerxes funded the rebuilding of the walls and appointed Nehemiah as governor of Judea. Nehemiah was able to personally oversee the restoration effort, and both he and Ezra worked for the reconciliation of Jews with Persian rule. Artaxerxes also allowed the Jews to freely practice and develop their religion and culture. His efforts earned him a considerable section in the Bible.

The conflicting reports in historical accounts, which show Artaxerxes first deciding against the Jews before supporting them, have raised some questions. Many believe the first incidence, the narration of the rebuilding of the city walls and the construction of the beams for the temple being halted by "Artaxerxes," may not have referred to the Persian king but instead to a usurper, who may have manipulated his way to the throne before Artaxerxes. However, no historical records reflect either the rule or the existence of such a person, and it may simply be that Artaxerxes had not known the true situation in Jerusalem before ordering the temple construction to be stopped.

After Artaxerxes

During his reign, Artaxerxes focused his efforts on much besides war and strife. The city of Susa held most of his favor, as he introduced a lot of developments in the region. He ordered the restoration of the palace of Darius I, which was destroyed in a fire, along with the building of many other temples. He also took up his father's work and finished construction on the Hall of a Hundred Columns.

Artaxerxes had already appointed his son, Xerxes II, as his heir to the throne by the time he died of natural causes in 424 BCE. Xerxes II was not fated to rule long, for hardly a month later, he was assassinated by his half-brother, Sogdianus, Artaxerxes's illegitimate son.

Sogdianus managed to gain the support of some of the nobles of Artaxerxes's court and was able to establish his rule. However, six months later, he, too, was assassinated. Ochus, his half-brother, went on to take the name Darius II. What is considered to have been the rule of a peace-loving emperor came to a violent end.

Chapter 8: Darius II and the Persian Involvement in the Peloponnesian War

The Persian Empire had been rapidly declining since the failed Persian expedition into Greece, which resulted in a humiliating defeat and heavy losses. The succession to the Persian throne had continued to grow increasingly violent, and each instance brought about new problems; nearly every change on the throne resulted in revolts across the empire. While these revolts were never a united action and were always suppressed, they brought increasing instability to the Persian Empire.

While Darius II was the son of Artaxerxes, his status as an illegitimate son made him, in the eyes of many, unworthy of the throne. Darius II was an unpopular ruler before his reign even began. He also had many challenges to face. Once again, the Egyptian subjects had risen up in rebellion, and the Greek threat continued to be a cause for concern.

Early Life and Ascension to the Throne

Minted coins of Darius II.

Darius II, whose original name was Ochus, was also often referred to as Nothus, meaning "bastard." His violent ascension to the throne did not bode well for the empire. Historians note that the Achaemenid court fell into rapid decline with his rule, as tensions, strife, and conflicts became commonplace. While he was the illegitimate son of Artaxerxes, his manner of obtaining the throne caused much unrest in the empire and became a hallmark of his reign.

After becoming king in 423 BCE, the focus of Darius II's life is reported to have been influenced by eunuchs and his harem. His wife, Parysatis, was believed to hold great sway over him. Darius II relied heavily on her counsel, and she held much sway over the Persian court, using a network of spies loyal to her.

Parysatis is believed to have ordered the execution of a number of dissenters or individuals she believed to be a threat to her power over the throne. She is also credited as the one who made Darius II's rule over Persia possible. She is believed to have held land in Media, Babylon, and Syria and extorted money in the form of taxation. Much of Darius II's rule was punctuated by unrest and claims of corruption.

The Peloponnesian War

While the Peace of Callias prevented any further fighting between the Persians and the Athenians, Darius II did not honor the treaty. In 413 BCE, Athens suffered a major defeat at the hands of the Spartans in Syracuse. Seeing an opportunity, Darius II decided to launch an attack on the Greeks. He believed it was time to take back control of the regions of Asia Minor that had fallen under Athenian command.

He ordered the satraps of Asia Minor, Tissaphernes and Pharnabazus, to begin collecting overdue taxes in the region and to forge an alliance with the Spartans to help him topple Athenian power.

Enter the Spartans

The beginning of the Peloponnesian War went mostly in the favor of Athens. The Spartans were unable to break the power of the Athenians or dismantle the Delian League. However, poor military decision-making on the part of Athens led to the Spartans gaining the upper hand. The Athenians had funded the Egyptian revolt, diverting considerable resources from their ongoing conflict with Sparta. When the revolt failed, they launched an attack on Cyprus, once again using up resources without seeing any results.

These moves resulted in a weakened Athenian force, and they were dealt a heavy blow at Syracuse. Using the mutual dislike of Athens as a weapon, Darius II created an alliance with Sparta, resulting in an official agreement in 412 BCE. Following Athens's losses at Sicily against Sparta, Syracuse, and Corinth, both the Spartans and Persians believed Athens could be easily defeated, once and for all, through the alliance.

Darius II and Tissaphernes dictated that the Spartans and Persians would jointly continue the war against Athens under the condition that no peace treaty could be reached with Athens without the consent of both parties. The treaty also stated that any enemy of one party would become an enemy of the other, effectively solidifying a joint defensive stance.

The treaty also laid out another common objective for the Spartans and the Persians. In addition to defeating the Athenians, the alliance was to prevent the Athenians from furthering their interests. This included but was not limited to preventing Athenians from obtaining wealth or resources from lands they had taken from either the Persians or the Spartans.

This first treaty was rejected by the Spartans. The treaty stated that the Spartans would surrender all regions outside of the Peloponnese, but the Spartans had begun the war to liberate Greece from Athenian influence, which had grown immensely because of its leadership role in the Delian League. Sparta still sought an agreement with the Persians and asked for a revision to the terms.

The second treaty that was presented before Darius II and the Spartans set out similar terms but with a few additions and revisions. It stated clearly that any lands under the dominion of Darius II were off-limits to the Spartans. Similarly, any lands under Spartan rule were forbidden to the Persians.

Both parties were to provide assistance and aid to the other if and when such help was needed. The condition of war against the Athenians remained, including the condition of initiating peace with them. The treaty made a new addition that required the Spartans and the Persians to aid the other should one party face a rebellion or uprising from among their respective territories.

This second treaty was seen as simply clarifying the terms of the first one. To the Spartans, it was still not good enough. The promise laid out in the treaty of the Persian king rewarding the Spartans for their service seemed a moot point, as custom dictated Persian kings to do so for anyone who had done them a service. Moreover, the second treaty forbade the Spartans from creating a new empire following the Athenian defeat, which was unacceptable to the Spartans. They asked for another revision.

In late 411 BCE, the final treaty was presented to the two parties. This time, the treaty clarified that the lands under the rule of either party were their own, and each was free to do with them as they pleased. It also included payment for the material support the Spartans were providing, including ships, should they choose to receive it.

The treaty featured a significant negotiation. Darius II agreed to surrender the Greek regions of Macedonia, Thrace, Boeotia, Attica, and Thessaly once they had been recovered from the Athenians. He was also to send a fleet to the Spartans; in exchange, the Spartans promised that they would lay no claim to Greek regions in Asia Minor.

Once again, the treaty required the Spartans to give up the idea of liberating Greece. However, they were in a difficult position. The Athenian loss at Syracuse had presented a great opportunity; if they could deal a heavy blow with the might of the Persians, the Spartans could guarantee victory. On the other hand, the Persians had no strategic need for the Spartans since their greatest threat, Amorges, the leader of the Carian rebellion against Persia, had been suppressed.

The treaty held little meaning in the beginning and was not honored, for the most part, by the Persians, largely due to Tissaphernes, who did not offer the Spartans much assistance. Because of this, the Spartans felt they could attempt peace talks with Athens. However, once Darius II removed Tissaphernes as satrap and installed his son, Cyrus the Younger, in his place, the Spartans received much greater support from the Persians.

The Outcome of the Peloponnesian War

As the Peloponnesian War continued, the Athenians faced a much stronger foe in Sparta. While Athens's resources were rapidly depleting, Sparta had the support of the Persians and could engage in drawn-out battles. With the Persian fleet provided to the Spartans, they were able to gain some decisive victories. The Spartans built a fort in Attica, from where they could launch constant attacks on the Athenian countryside.

In 406 BCE, the Spartans were able to defeat Athens at the Battle of Notium in a naval confrontation. Despite an Athenian victory the same year, in 405 BCE, the Spartans defeated the Athenians, once and for all, at the Battle of Aegospotami. The Athenian fleet was captured, and Athens eventually surrendered, ending the Peloponnesian War in 404 BCE.

Following the war, Greece changed dramatically. It brought about the end of the once-powerful city-state of Athens and changed Greek warfare forever. The monetary and weaponry support provided by the Persians played a notable role in securing a Spartan victory, and it would go on to have a direct influence on dismantling the ruling influence of Athens. About sixty-six years later, Greece would be conquered by the Macedonian kingdom.

The Carian Rebellion

The rebellion that broke out in Caria in western Anatolia was led by Amorges in 413 BCE. When he rose up against Darius II, he was able to gain the sympathy and support of the Athenians. With this alliance, the Athenians hoped to weaken Persian rule, which, in turn, would hinder the support they were providing the Spartans, tipping the scales in favor of the Athenians. When the rebellion broke out, Tissaphernes was ordered to suppress the usurpers.

Since the Spartans were in a treaty with the Persians, they had to treat Amorges and the other rebels as their enemies. The Spartans set sail to Iasos, which had been occupied by the rebels between 412 to 411 BCE. The rebels celebrated their arrival, believing them to be the Athenian navy. However, they soon realized their mistake. The Spartans fought and defeated Amorges's army, arresting him and handing him over to Tissaphernes.

Background to the Egyptian Revolt

The previous Egyptian revolts had made the situation precarious in the region well before Darius II's violent ascension to the throne. Another rebellion began, this time with a more decisive outcome. After the Egyptian revolt during Artaxerxes I's reign, a new satrap, Arsames, was installed in Egypt. He chose to adopt a conciliatory approach with the hope of discouraging any new rebellion that might spring up. Part of his approach to managing Egypt was allowing Thannyras, Inaros's son, to maintain his lordship.

When Darius II obtained the throne, Arsames supported and pledged allegiance to him. Reportedly, between the years of 410 BCE and 407 BCE, Arsames was called out of Egypt to Susa. At the same time, a revolt broke out in Egypt.

The Egyptian Revolt

In 410 BCE, the region of Elephantine became the focal point of a revolt. Tensions between the Jewish community of Elephantine and the native Egyptians living there rose. Artaxerxes I had established a policy of religious tolerance across the Persian Empire, and various communities lived in relative harmony.

However, reports indicate that some strife was caused by the Jewish practice of sacrificing goats. The Egyptians saw this as an insult and took advantage of Arsames's absence to bribe a local military leader into destroying the Jewish temple. It is reported that Arsames punished the people responsible for the destruction, but to remain fair, he also banned the sacrifices, ignoring the pleas from the Jews.

The true cause and evolution of the revolt are not known for certain. Amyrtaeus, the pharaoh of the Twenty-eighth Egyptian dynasty, led a rebellion against the Persian Empire, with the rebellion reportedly starting as early as 411 BCE. The revolt led to guerilla attacks along the Nile Delta, which was taken out of Persian control by the rebels.

Amyrtaeus's grandfather may have participated in an earlier rebellion in Egypt. However, this time, Amyrtaeus sought help from the Spartans and forged an alliance. The Spartans were to engage the Persians in a conflict in Asia in exchange for Egyptian grain. This would turn Persian attention away from Egypt.

Reports vary on just how successful the revolt was. After the death of Darius II, Amyrtaeus was able to instate himself as the pharaoh of Egypt. Yet it appears Amyrtaeus may have only gained control of the Nile Delta at this point, with Upper Egypt remaining under Persian control. Darius II's successor, Artaxerxes II, was able to gather an army to lead a charge against the rebels soon after taking the throne. Political unrest at home and the threat of civil war prevented him from taking timely action, though. Eventually, the Egyptians were able to overthrow Achaemenid rule and declare independence.

The End of Darius II

Darius II died from an illness in 404 BCE. He was succeeded by his son, Artaxerxes II, who faced an increasingly struggling empire. He also faced internal struggles, as his younger brother, Cyrus the Younger, harbored ambitions for the Persian throne since his appointment as satrap of Persian-occupied regions of Greece. Cyrus had even reportedly hoped to enlist the help of the Spartans since he had been responsible for providing them aid during the Peloponnesian War.

The Legacy of Darius II

Darius II's role in the Peloponnesian War is considered a cunning example of military strategy. By identifying a true moment of opportunity, Darius was able to forge an alliance with the Spartans, which would go on to secure their victory against the Athenians. The Athenians, who had been defeated by the Persians at Cyprus, had already been weakened, and Darius II was able to make use of their weakened state and the Spartans' desire to overthrow them to ultimately destroy one of Persia's enemies. The continued fighting between the Greeks ensured they would be too occupied to launch attacks, at least any truly threatening attacks, on the Persians. The civil war could also pave the way for the Persians to take over Greece.

By using the alliance with the Spartans, Darius II was also able to overthrow Amorges, quashing the Carian rebellion and eliminating a true threat to the Persian Empire. However, regardless of his success, much of Darius II's rule was punctuated by rebellions, revolts, and general unrest. By the end of his rule, the Persians had to give up their regions in Greece and had lost many parts of Egypt, which were never regained again. The influence and corruption of Darius's wife caused unrest within the Persian court.

Aside from his campaigns, Darius II contributed to the religion, language, and culture of the Persian Empire. During his reign, he was able to bring back and mandate the use of three primary languages: Babylonian, Elamite, and Old Persian. Much of the writings recovered from this period were recorded in Elamite, which also served as the government's official language.

He continued to support and practice Zoroastrianism, paying tribute to Ahura Mazda, the creator deity in Zoroastrianism. Ancient records show Darius II was a great believer in spiritual and supernatural forces and maintained a collection of monuments with spiritual inscriptions on them. His tomb also showcases many such carvings.

PART THREE:
THE PERSIANS – THE ROAD
TO COLLAPSE

Chapter 9: Artaxerxes II: A Troubled Period

Following the death of Darius II, the Persian Empire came under the rule of his son, Artaxerxes II. By this point, the Persians had faced success in their funding of the Spartans during the Peloponnesian War, cultivating a strategic alliance with them as Athenian power was broken. With the threat of Athens vanquished, regions across the Aegean fell back under Persian rule, reestablishing, to some degree, the might of the Achaemenid Empire.

On the other hand, Artaxerxes II also inherited a revolt in Egypt, which had been stirring toward the end of his father's rule. The new king's reign would be marked with civil unrest and revolts, and the war waged on him by his brother in a bid for the throne would leave a lasting impression on the future of Persia.

About Artaxerxes II

Artaxerxes II.

Artaxerxes II, also known as Arsaces, was one of Darius II and Parysatis's thirteen children. He came to the throne in 424 BCE. His succession was contested by his younger brother, Cyrus, who may also have had the support of their mother, Parysatis. Cyrus had been appointed satrap of Lydia and other regions in Asia Minor under Persian control. When Tissaphernes failed to provide the promised amount of support to the Spartans during the Peloponnesian War, he was replaced with Cyrus the Younger. This position, along with his title of "Karanos," which denoted a higher rank than that of an ordinary satrap, greatly extended his military and political autonomy.

It was perhaps for this reason that Cyrus expected to be appointed heir to the throne. Many historians believe he was favored by his mother, who was known to hold great influence over her husband. However, Darius II appointed Arsaces as his heir on his deathbed. Upon Arsaces's acquisition of the throne, he adopted the royal title of Artaxerxes II.

Reports of hostilities between the brothers suggest that Cyrus may have attempted to assassinate his brother during his coronation. However, there is no real account of such an event occurring. Even if Artaxerxes II's coronation had gone smoothly, the remainder of his reign was marked with feuds, revolts, and unrest.

Blood Feud: Artaxerxes vs. Cyrus

As satrap, Cyrus managed to amass a large army and forge close alliances. His victory against the Cilicians and Syrians had given him great military prowess. He laid claim to the Persian throne immediately after hearing the news of his father's death. He believed he was the rightful heir. Although he was not the oldest, he was the firstborn after Darius II became king, whereas Artaxerxes had been born before his rule began.

Artaxerxes II's attempts at reaching a peaceful resolution did not come to any viable end. To aid his claim to the throne, Cyrus gathered his troops, composed of Lydian and Ionian soldiers and Greek mercenaries. Cyrus's plans were realized by Tissaphernes, who found flaws in the former's apparent excuse that he was gathering forces to launch an attack on the Pisidians in Asia Minor. His suspicion was solidified when Cyrus sought political support for his campaign from the Spartans and managed to receive funding from the Cilicians, whom he had conquered. Tissaphernes relayed his suspicions to the king, and Artaxerxes II began to prepare for a confrontation.

What occurred next was a bloody clash between the two brothers, with Cyrus leading a large army called the "Ten Thousand." This confrontation produced mixed results and led to more trouble.

Battle of Cunaxa

Cyrus the Younger's revolt came to a head in 401 BCE at Cunaxa near Babylon. Cyrus's army was led by a Spartan general named Clearchus. Artaxerxes II prepared an army four times the strength of Cyrus's, which was led by Ariaeus, his second-in-command. Accounts from one historian, who fought as a Greek soldier in the battle, report that Cyrus may not have had much control over his army. Reportedly, Cyrus wanted the Greeks, whom he deemed to be his best fighters, to take the center, where they would be in the best position to defeat the cavalry and kill the Persian king. The Greeks refused to do so, believing it would weaken their position.

When the battle began, the Spartans charged the left of Artaxerxes's army. They were heavily outnumbered and unable to break through, eventually breaking rank and fleeing. However, the Greek mercenaries were able to advance farther, forcing the Persians to fall back. By military standards, Cyrus's army was able to exact a defeat on the Persians, despite their fewer numbers. However, Cyrus was killed during the battle by a flying javelin, thus rendering the victory pointless.

The War with Sparta

The Spartan support of Cyrus during his rebellion went directly against the terms of the agreement the Spartans had signed with the Persians. Their betrayal angered Artaxerxes II, who wanted to act against them. The main conflict between the two powers began with the Corinthian War in 395 BCE. The Spartan invasion of Asia Minor, which was under Persian control, made the Persian king realize the Spartan threat needed to be neutralized immediately. To divert Sparta's attention from Persia, Artaxerxes began a mass political campaign, which involved heavy bribery, to encourage Sparta's enemies, including the Thebans, Corinthians, and Athenians, to begin a war with Sparta.

His strategy was successful, and Sparta became preoccupied with attacks on multiple fronts. It also led to an alliance, albeit a temporary one, between Persia and Athens. The two nations levied a joint attack on Sparta after failed peace negotiations. The ensuing Battle of Cnidus dealt a heavy blow to the Spartans, allowing Athens to make a comeback.

Battle of Cnidus

In 394 BCE, the Persians and the Athenians joined together to face off against the Spartan navy. Sparta's attempt to establish its newly built navy, which the Spartans began to build in 413 BCE, as a formidable force was led by King Agesilaus II of Sparta, who was recalled from Ionia to fight the Persian-Athenian threat. The combined navy of the latter was led by Athenian admiral Conon and Persian satrap Pharnabazus II.

The Spartan fleet met an advance guard of the Achaemenid fleet, against which the Spartans met relative success. But with the arrival of the remainder of the Persian fleet, the Spartans were hard put to resist. They were forced to abandon many ships and suffered massive casualties, with the Persians reportedly capturing at least fifty Spartan triremes. Although the Corinthian War continued, Sparta did not engage in naval conflicts after this defeat, which left the arena open for Athens to establish its naval power.

The allied forces of Persia and Athens raided the coast of the Peloponnese, which was under Spartan control, increasing the pressure on the Spartans. Persia was able to regain Ionia and its lost regions of the Aegean. This control was formally established with the Peace of Antalcidas, which began in 387 BCE.

The Resurgence of Athens

The Peloponnesian War had left Sparta as the reigning force in Greece, bringing Athenian supremacy in the region to an end. However, with Sparta's might breaking during the Corinthian War, especially with their defeat at Cnidus, Athens saw an opportunity to build itself back up. Athenian ambitions came to the attention of Artaxerxes, who feared that Athens would move against Asia Minor and strike up another war with the Persians.

As a result, Artaxerxes II sought a peace treaty with Sparta, which was, of course, seen as a betrayal to Athens. The Peace of Antalcidas was between the Greeks and the Persian king, and it restored peace and the Anatolian regions to the Persians. It also allowed Sparta to regain its dominance on the mainland.

The King's Peace

The Peace of Antalcidas is also known as the King's Peace since it was settled by Artaxerxes II. While it originated from the threat Athens posed to the Persian Empire, it ended the Corinthian War. The peace treaty allowed Athens to maintain its dominion in the regions of Lemnos, Imbros, and Scyros and granted autonomy to other regions.

Since the Persians made the treaty possible and brought peace to the region, the Persians became arbitrators of future Greek conflicts. This status would go on to play a significant role in resolving conflicts between the Spartans and the Thebans.

Mediation between Sparta and Thebes

The King's Peace did not hold for long, and fighting resumed in Greece. Thebes, in particular, faced resentment from other Greek city-states on account of the level of influence it held within Greece. Between 367 and 365 BCE, further attempts were made to restore peace to the region, with Artaxerxes II acting as a neutral and fair arbiter. However, Theban attempts at organizing peace talks failed completely, especially when Thebes refused to return conquered Spartan land. The result was a continuation of fighting in Greece.

During the peace negotiations, Artaxerxes used an envoy, Philiscus, to act on his behalf. The failure of the peace talks led Philiscus to begin offering Persian funds to the Spartan military, offering them moral and monetary support. Records suggest he also funded the Athenian army and may have offered them services since he was named an Athenian citizen. With the Achaemenid Empire's backing, the war in Greece could continue.

The failure of negotiations was not well received by any of the Greek city-states. In 367 BCE, the Spartans and later the Athenians, as well as the Thebans and other city-states, sent envoys to the Achaemenid court, hoping to gain Artaxerxes's support to fund their war effort. Artaxerxes II proposed a new treaty that would theoretically end the war. However, it was perceived by all to be heavily in favor of Thebes, as it required the dismantling of other militaries. As a result, most city-states, aside from Thebes, rejected the proposal.

Artaxerxes II's apparent favoritism for the Thebans enraged the other states, who began to act against the Persian Empire in secret. Athens and Sparta began to offer military support to known enemies of Persia. As a result, both Athens and Sparta became involved in the Egyptian revolt, as well as the Revolt of the Satraps.

The Egyptian Attempt

With the Greek threat suppressed, Artaxerxes finally turned his attention to Egypt. Toward the end of his father's rule and the beginning of his own, Egypt had launched a successful revolt, taking delta regions out of Persian control and establishing a new pharaoh. While Upper Egypt remained under Persian control, the revolt was not satiated and required urgent action. Artaxerxes II's first attempt to subjugate the Egyptians in 385 BCE did not end well, so he turned to the Greeks for aid. He began recruiting Greek mercenaries and led an invasion into Egypt in 373 BCE.

Due to Pharnabazus's success against the Spartans, he was chosen to lead the attack on Egypt. After four years of preparation, Pharnabazus had a 200,000-strong military force backed by 12,000 Greeks and naval support, the latter of whom marched under Iphicrates, a Greek general, to face the Egyptian rebels in 373 BCE. The Egyptians were supported by an Athenian general named Chabrias, who brought many Greek mercenaries with him.

The Egyptians were prepared for the oncoming Persian force and placed the lands around Pelusium, to which the Persians were headed, underwater and blocked all available channels of the Nile by building embankments. Finding the heavily fortified Nile impassable, the Persian army had to move on from Pelusium without attempting an attack and look for an alternate way up the Nile.

The Persians then headed toward Memphis, finding a route through the sparsely guarded Mendesian channel of the Nile River. However, luck was against the Persians, as disagreements between Iphicrates and Pharnabazus, combined with the Nile flooding, created tensions. The fortifications and the attack put up by the Egyptians turned a certain victory into a sour defeat. Pharnabazus was later removed from his military duties due to his advanced age and was replaced by another general, Datames, who was to lead a second expedition into Egypt. Not only would this second campaign fail, but it also led to Datames leading the Revolt of the Satraps against the Achaemenid king.

Revolt of the Satraps

Repeated revolts and the utter defeat in Egypt led to increasing unrest in an already struggling empire. Starting in 372 BCE, the nobility of the Achaemenid dynasty revolted. They were led by Datames. While he was initially appointed to command the second expedition into Egypt, he changed his mind, instead turning against the Persian emperor. He and his troops withdrew from Egypt and headed to Cappadocia, where he was able to confer and ally himself with other displeased satraps.

This revolt within Persia, which would undoubtedly weaken it and render it unable to mount attacks or defenses against other enemies, offered a golden opportunity to the rebels in Egypt. Egyptian Pharaoh Nectanebo, who had been leading the assault against the Persians, lent support to the satraps in the form of financial aid and began cultivating ties with both Athens and Sparta.

The satraps planned to lead an assault against the Achaemenid king, starting with an attack from Syria, while an Egyptian-Greek alliance launched an attack from the southwest. While the satraps began their revolt as intended, the Egyptian army never came to their aid, as it was waylaid by the Egyptian revolt. Disagreements and infighting among the satraps led to an uncoordinated and messy attack against the Persian king, and he was able to defeat the rebels without much loss. However, to maintain peace within his empire, Artaxerxes II allowed many of the satraps to return to their governorship.

Persia Starts to Crumble

During his reign, Artaxerxes II spent a considerable portion of his wealth on several building projects. These included the restoration of the palace of Darius I and stronger fortifications in Susa. In Ecbatana, he funded the building of a new palace and several sculptures. A notable change in Persian culture during his reign was the growth of religion. While the Persian Empire was dominated by the Zoroastrian faith, which worshiped Ahura Mazda, the names of other gods were also recovered that date to Artaxerxes II's reign. These include Anahita and Mithra, who were lesser gods worshiped in conjunction with Ahura Mazda.

Artaxerxes II was the first of the Persian kings to recognize these two deities. Anahita was associated with healing, fertility, and wisdom. Artaxerxes erected temples, which were populated by statues of the goddesses across the empire, particularly in Babylon, Susa, and Ecbatana.

Despite such advances, the general view of Artaxerxes II is that of an inept ruler who reigned over an empire in constant conflict. He was unable to control the rising tensions, which finally erupted into war. Egypt was lost during his reign. His rule is highlighted not by the empire's expansion but by a constant struggle to maintain peace and control over the existing regions under Persian rule. The Achaemenid dynasty faced many complications during Artaxerxes II's reign, each with a lasting effect. The war Artaxerxes II waged against Cyrus the Younger is even believed to have laid the groundwork for future conflicts, particularly the Revolt of the Satraps.

Artaxerxes II died in 358 BCE and was succeeded by his son, Artaxerxes III. His successor did not inherit the region in any better condition than Artaxerxes II had, so he was destined to face similar challenges during his rule. Artaxerxes II was buried in his tomb in Persepolis.

Chapter 10: Artaxerxes III: The Instability Continues

During Artaxerxes II's reign, the Persian Empire struggled. It faced many challenges, and revolts broke out throughout the empire. Artaxerxes II's ineptitude in dealing with and suppressing these revolts left room for his successor to be perceived as weak if he could not restore peace. So, Artaxerxes III came to the throne with a clear ambition.

Under the new king, the Persian Empire saw a series of effective military operations designed to ensure that the empire would not fall apart. Artaxerxes III's ruthlessness and military strategy made him an effective emperor. While the foundation of the Achaemenid dynasty was shaky, it held on under the watchful and brutal eye of Artaxerxes III.

Taking the Throne

Artaxerxes III.

Bruce Allardice, CC BY-SA 2.0 <https://creativecommons.org/licenses/by-sa/2.0>, via Wikimedia Commons; https://commons.wikimedia.org/wiki/File:Artaxerxes_III_tomb_detail.jpg

Despite not being the next in line for the throne, Ochus, otherwise known as Artaxerxes III, ascended to the throne following his father's death in 358 BCE. Before beginning his reign over the Persian Empire, he served as a satrap and a military commander in the Persian army. Of Ochus's three brothers, any of whom could have inherited the throne, one committed suicide, another was executed, and the third was murdered. This type of violent pattern was to follow the entirety of Artaxerxes III's reign.

Artaxerxes II's oldest son, Darius, had been in line for the throne, and he was favored by the king. However, to quicken his succession, he began plotting against his father, hoping to gain the support of his half-brothers, his father's illegitimate children, rumored to be around 150 in number. The treachery was discovered, and Darius was executed. Next in line was Ariaspes, who, through clever manipulation from Ochus, was pushed into committing suicide. Artaxerxes II's other choice was his favorite illegitimate son Arsames, as he disliked Ochus and did not wish him to accede to the throne. However, Ochus had Arsames killed. Artaxerxes II died soon after finally appointing Ochus as the next king of Persia.

Artaxerxes III began his rule with major bloodshed within the royal family. To quash the potential of any other contender for the throne or anyone challenging the legitimacy of his rule, he murdered all the members of the royal family, including women and children, to secure the throne. He came to be known as one of the cruelest Persian kings. Through cunning, manipulation, and extreme violence, he conducted multiple campaigns in Egypt. He also led a defensive charge against the Greeks, who rose up against Achaemenid rule, and dealt with multiple other rebellions during his rule.

Artabazus Revolts

The Revolt of the Satraps during Artaxerxes II's reign made his son, Artaxerxes III, realize the threat the nobility presented to the throne. It wasn't all that long ago that Cyrus the Younger had engaged in a civil war to win the throne instead of Artaxerxes II. Artaxerxes III was adamant about avoiding such a situation. For this reason, after becoming king, he required all satraps to disassemble their personal mercenary forces.

Initially, the satraps complied with this order. However, two years later, Artaxerxes III's attempt to remove Artabazus II from his governorship of Hellespontine Phrygia in western Anatolia did not go as planned. Artabazus did not appreciate the dismissal and chose to revolt against the Persian king instead. He also happened to be the son of the king's sister, which may have made him particularly hostile toward Artaxerxes III since he would have seen the discharge as an insult. During the Revolt of the Satraps during Artaxerxes II's reign, Artabazus led the resistance for the king and had been ultimately victorious in suppressing the rebellion. He is believed to have joined forces with his two brothers to lead this new revolt.

To counter the force Artaxerxes III sent against him, which included all the other satraps of Anatolia, Artabazus reached out to the Athenians for help. He was able to forge an alliance with the Athenian commander, Chares, who obtained the mercenaries Artabazus was forced to dismiss two years prior. This combined force was able to defeat the satrap force sent by Artaxerxes III. The king saw the greater danger posed by the Athenians and bribed them to remove themselves from the Persian conflict.

In response, Artabazus formed an alliance with the Thebans in 354 BCE, who supplied him with a military force to face off against the Persian king. For a while, it seemed the former satrap had the upper hand, as he was able to inflict defeat on the Achaemenid king multiple times. Artabazus's downfall came from within, as he had a falling out with the Theban general. Artabazus was defeated in battle and taken prisoner. His supporters were able to free him, and after a few half-hearted attempts to continue the revolt, he fled to Macedonia to the court of Philip II. His arrival in Macedonia proved to be significant, as this was where he met his future son-in-law, Alexander the Great.

Failure in Egypt

Artaxerxes II's defeat in Egypt and his failure to control the rebellion turned into a point of humiliation and contention within the empire, which later led to the Revolt of the Satraps. His son wanted to fix this situation and earn respect and the credit of bringing an unruly satrapy back under Persian dominion. Artaxerxes III is reported to have launched a new campaign against the Egyptians around 351 BCE, hoping to finally put an end to years of war.

Little is known about this campaign. Artaxerxes III is believed to have marched into Egypt with a huge army and directly engaged Pharoah Nectanebo II. The Egyptians had the support of both the Athenians and the Spartans. This allied force dealt a deceive defeat to the Persians after reportedly a year of fighting, at which point Artaxerxes III was forced to abandon the Egyptian campaign to address more urgent matters at hand—another revolt.

The Cyprus Campaign

Cyprus, like Egypt, had a history of rebelling against the Persian Empire, though they had been repressed successfully in the past. During Artaxerxes II's reign, Evagoras, the king of Salamis, attempted a revolt, seeking to gain all of Cyprus.

With Artaxerxes II occupied by his brother Cyrus the Younger's attempt at seizing the throne, Evagoras secured the support of Athens and Egypt. Victory seemed inevitable for the rebels. However, the King's Peace with Athens meant Greek support was withdrawn, and the Cypriot revolt came to an end.

During Artaxerxes III's reign, Cyprus revolted again, seeking independence from Persia. Unfortunately for Cyprus, victory was still out of reach. With the help of its allies, the Persian Empire was able to, once again, suppress the uprising. Cyprus would eventually gain independence from the Persian Empire, but it remained part of the empire under the rule of Artaxerxes III.

The Defeat of Sidon

More rebellions sprang up. The Phoenicians in Sidon were tired of Persian rule as well. To handle the rebellion of Sidon, Artaxerxes III reached out to the satraps of Syria and Cilicia, Belesys and Mazaeus, respectively. The Persian forces might have been something to reckon with were it not for the support of Egypt, which sent four thousand Greek mercenaries to help Phoenicia gain independence from the Persian Empire. The satraps' army failed to deal with the rebellion and was driven out of Phoenicia. The failure of the satraps in Phoenicia led Artaxerxes III to reconsider this decision.

Following this failure, Artaxerxes III decided to lead an army himself into Sidon. Both the Athenians and the Spartans refused to provide aid to the Persian army, but he was able to secure aid from the Thebans, who added another 10,000 men to the 330,000-strong army Artaxerxes III had gathered. The king hoped to cripple the revolt by sheer force since his army far outnumbered the Phoenicians.

The outcome of the campaign against Sidon provides a look into the viciousness and barbarity of which Artaxerxes III is often accused. The strength of the Persian force worried the king of Sidon, Tennes, who led the rebellion. He decided to seek the king's pardon by offering one hundred influential citizens of Sidon. Artaxerxes responded by having each citizen speared with javelins. An additional tribute of five hundred citizens met the same fate.

Artaxerxes III then set about burning the city to the ground, killing about forty thousand people in the process. He went on to make a fortune from his victory by selling the ruins of the city to those who believed there were vast treasures to be found buried underneath it, which they hoped to excavate from the ashes. Tennes was executed for instigating the uprising, and the Jews who had supported the rebellion were exiled to Hyrcania.

Reconquering Egypt

Artaxerxes III spent many years preparing for reentry into Egypt. Between 340 and 339 BCE, he assembled a large army consisting of mercenaries recruited from Argos, Thebes, and Asia Minor. The Persians' challenge was not the strength of their army; indeed, the Persian force had always greatly outnumbered the Egyptian forces. The treacherous terrain was the problem. The Persians' limited knowledge of Egyptian topography and their arrogant refusal to recruit a local guide exacerbated the problem.

The Egyptian climate did impact the Persians, who were bested by quicksand. Their hasty attempt to take Pelusium was also quickly vanquished. Artaxerxes III then changed strategies, dividing up his troops into three divisions. The Theban division was assigned Pelusium. The Mentor of Rhodes, a Greek mercenary, was tasked with the campaign against Bubastis in Egypt, and the final division, made up of Argive troops, was to establish themselves against the Egyptians on the opposite bank of the Nile River.

The Egyptian ruler, Nectanebo II, was unable to dismantle the forces gathered on the opposite bank of the Nile and chose to retreat to Memphis. Pelusium, which was under siege by the Thebans, also fell, and Bubastis followed suit. The Greek mercenaries fighting for the Egyptians chose to surrender rather than face a brutal death at the hands of the Persians. They struck a deal with the Persians and defected, leading to widespread surrenders and allowing Artaxerxes to cross the Nile and reconquer Egypt. Nectanebo fled the country rather than face the Persians.

Egypt's fate was little better than that of Sidon. A reign of terror began; the city walls were destroyed, and the region was thoroughly looted by the Persians. The stolen riches greatly contributed to the Persian treasury and helped Artaxerxes reward his mercenaries. The king then set about weakening Egypt's people and the economy to prevent the likelihood of another revolt. Taxes were raised astronomically, and sacred books were burned. Temples were looted, and local religions were persecuted.

The Fall of Artaxerxes III

Egypt was not the last rebellion the Persian Empire faced, but it certainly had a lasting effect. Artaxerxes III continued his policy of vicious attacks in response to revolts, and within a few years of reconquering Egypt, he managed to subdue rebellions across the empire, bringing lands firmly back under Achaemenid control. Generals, including Mentor of Rhodes, who had played prominent and successful roles in the Egyptian campaign, were given important positions within the empire and worked to maintain Persian authority and create a successful and efficient government.

The Persian Empire regained control of the Aegean, including many of the Athenian regions. While the Greeks suffered from the might of the Persians, none were able to take a stand against them. However, the rising power of Macedonia remained a concern for Artaxerxes III. Persia became a focal point for Philip II of Macedonia when Persian aid helped Thrace topple the Macedonian siege and maintain independence.

The final years of Artaxerxes III's reign were spent in relative peace. In 338 BCE, Artaxerxes III and his elder sons were poisoned by a court eunuch named Bagoas. Bagoas ensured that a more malleable heir, one of the king's sons, Arses, ascended the throne. Artaxerxes III's sudden death wreaked havoc on an otherwise stable empire.

During his reign, Artaxerxes III built the Hall of Thirty-Two Columns for some unknown purpose and his own palace. However, many of his construction projects remained unfinished, including the Army Road and the Unfinished Gate, which would have connected the Hall of a Hundred Columns with the Gate of All Nations. His tomb was built next to his father's.

Chapter 11: Arses and Darius III: The Last Kings and the Dissolution of the Empire

Artaxerxes III managed to consolidate the Persian Empire largely by sheer force and unbridled violence. The empire had gone through one too many periods of unrest and had suffered considerably from external wars and internal rebellions. However, his death would spark unrest greater than the empire had seen before, leading to the complete decimation of the Achaemenid dynasty.

The last two rulers of the Persian Empire, Artaxerxes IV and Darius III, were unable to handle the demands of this vast and unstable kingdom. Their inability to do so may be attributed to several reasons, but the manner of their ascension played a large role. When Artaxerxes IV's rule began, the Persian Empire slowly came to an end.

Arses Takes the Throne: Artaxerxes IV

Artaxerxes IV.
*Classical Numismatic Group, Inc. http://www.cngcoins.com, CC BY-SA 3.0
<http://creativecommons.org/licenses/by-sa/3.0/>, via Wikimedia Commons;
https://commons.wikimedia.org/wiki/File:Artaxerxes_IV_portrait.jpg*

The youngest of Artaxerxes III's sons, Arses, was not first in line for the throne. The purposeful poisoning of Arses's father and his other siblings left him suddenly in charge of an empire he may not have been fit to rule. Arses was still young when he became king in 338 BCE, taking the throne name Artaxerxes IV. The general consensus behind Bagoas's acts is that by making young Arses king of an empire he could not manage alone, he could take charge behind the scenes by exerting influence on the new king. Artaxerxes IV would be more acceptable to the Persian court and the people rather than Bagoas directly attempting to take it.

The Rise of Macedonia

The political unrest in Persia gave its enemies a golden opportunity to make use of its weaknesses. Artaxerxes III vowed to keep a united empire and worked on subduing revolts and maintaining peace. During this time, he became aware of the rising threat of Philip II of Macedonia, particularly after the Persians aided Thrace against the Macedonians.

The Macedonian king had been gathering power and influence in Greece. Many Greek city-states had already joined Philip II in the League of Corinth, which was led by him. The Macedonian king, supported by his own influence and the faltering Persian Empire, chose the time of Artaxerxes IV's ascension to demand monetary compensation from the Persians. According to Philip, this compensation was owed because of what the Persians had cost the Macedonians by helping Thrace.

Artaxerxes IV refused to give in to the Macedonian ruler's demands. Philip II did not take this slight well and began to prepare for war, building up an army to enter Persia. However, Artaxerxes IV did not live long enough to meet the Macedonian threat.

The Reign of Artaxerxes IV

Little is known about Artaxerxes IV's reign. The main source of knowledge regarding the Persian Empire is ancient Greek historians, who took little interest in Achaemenid affairs at this time. Since Artaxerxes IV had little involvement in Greek affairs, historians were more preoccupied with events happening closer at hand. Few records speak of Artaxerxes IV's reign.

What is known is that Artaxerxes IV's rule did not strengthen the Persian Empire much. The Persians were struggling, with Egypt and Babylon both attempting to establish their independence. Meanwhile, the king was too preoccupied to deal with the Macedonians or the unrest within his empire.

Realizing how much ambition Bagoas held, Artaxerxes IV attempted to rid himself of the nuisance and traitor. He tried poisoning Bagoas, but the latter got there first. Artaxerxes IV was poisoned just two years after claiming the throne, bringing his rule to an end in 336 BCE. Bagoas proceeded to place the former king's distant cousin, Artashata, on the Persian throne.

Darius III Becomes King

Coin of Darius III.

Artashata was part of the Persian royal family, being a distant cousin to the previous king. Upon his ascension to the throne, he took the name Darius III. At this point, the Persian Empire had been considerably weakened, not because of outside attacks but because of internal instability, political threats, and a crumbling administration. Due to Bagoas's actions, the empire's focus had turned toward matters of succession and away from the management and security of a vast and rapidly deteriorating empire.

Reports suggest that Darius III may not have succumbed to Bagoas's influence easily. Bagoas attempted to poison the newly appointed king of the Persian Empire because of this or perhaps because of some other conflict. Historical accounts suggest Darius III discovered this treachery before it occurred and summoned Bagoas to his court. There, the king forced him to drink to the former's health from his cup, which had already been poisoned. Bagoas was pushed to consume his own poison and was killed.

Little is known about Darius III besides his rather flimsy connection with the royal family. He may have gained some recognition from his military career. He had been part of the Persian military since the reign of Artaxerxes III and is reported to have shown bravery during one of his campaigns. This achievement lifted him from obscurity, with the king making him the satrap of Armenia. However, his ascension to the throne may be more aptly attributed to the power-hungry actions of Bagoas than to Darius III's military aptitude. His main claim to fame is being the last ruler of the Persian Empire.

The Persians were completely distracted and blindsided by outside threats, which was a problem since Artaxerxes IV's offense had led to the Macedonian king, Philip II, gearing up for war. The Greeks prepared for yet another attack on the Persians. The Persian Empire's previous might had thwarted many such attempts before through force, strategy, alliance, and/or bribery. However, this time, the Persians were not prepared to put up any resistance when the Macedonians marched against them.

The Macedonian Campaign

Whether the Macedonians had already been planning an attack on Persia, perceiving it as weak, or whether it only came as a result of Artaxerxes IV's refusal to offer compensation is not clear. The reported revolts or unrest in Egypt and Babylon during this time may have demonstrated that Persia was unable to maintain the peace that

Artaxerxes III had worked so hard to establish. However, it is true that the Egyptian and Babylonian uprisings were not very significant, as little is mentioned about them in the historical records.

Regardless of how or why, Macedonia turned its eye to the Persian Empire. This rising force had gained great influence in Greece, and the League of Corinth had received substantial support. The league was assembled by Philip II, and its express purpose was to unite the military forces of the various Greek city-states against the Achaemenid Empire.

The First Charge

By 336 BCE, Philip II had received the full support of the League of Corinth to lead a charge against the Persian Empire. The charge was supposed to be revenge for the acts of barbarianism the Persians had committed during the second Persian invasion of Greece when they desecrated many Athenian temples, even though the offense had occurred a century ago and under a different ruler.

Philip II sent an advance force to Asia Minor with the goal of liberating the Greeks from Persian rule. This first campaign was successful, and the Macedonians were able to reclaim cities stretching from Troy to the Malandros River. The campaign may have continued were it not for Philip's unexpected death. He was stabbed by one of his bodyguards as he entered the town of Aegae to celebrate his daughter's marriage. He had arrived unprotected to appear friendly and approachable to the citizens. It is not known for sure why he was stabbed, although there are many stories about why people might have been upset with him.

Alexander the Great Arrives

Alexander the Great was already a seasoned warrior in the Macedonian military when his father was assassinated in 336 BCE. When he ascended the throne, he also became the leader of the League of Corinth. Two years later, he led an invasion into Asia Minor with allied armies made up of Macedonian and Greek soldiers. The threat of Alexander was vastly underestimated by the Persians.

Battle of the Granicus

The reported Egyptian revolt had taken priority for the Persian emperor, who turned his attention away from the looming Macedonian threat. When Darius III turned back toward the approaching Macedonian army, he did not believe it to be any great danger. He appointed his satrap with the task of dealing with the Greeks and refused to personally engage in battle.

The Persian army was able to defeat the Macedonian forces twice, in Magnesia and again in Troad in Asia Minor. The advance guard that had been sent by Philip II the previous year, which had acquired various regions of Asia Minor, lost its command, and the lands were restored to Persian control.

The satraps' initial success made Darius III confident in their abilities to defeat Alexander the Great. The Persian army was led by the satraps of Hellespontine Phrygia, Lydia, and Cilicia. The Persian army took the western bank of the Granicus River, where they waited for the Macedonians, who took the opposing bank.

The Persians likely thought they were favored to win. The Persians were fighting from higher ground and outnumbered Alexander's army, being almost twice its size. However, the Macedonians soon gained the upper hand, which is largely attributed to their more effective weaponry, particularly their lances. During the battle, Alexander killed Darius III's son-in-law, Mithridates.

Alexander's army was able to push the Persian forces back, gaining a strong foothold on the riverbank. Much of the Persian cavalry abandoned the battle and fled, though Alexander did not pursue them. Those who remained behind were defeated and captured. Alexander erected the Granicus Monument to commemorate his first major victory over the Persians.

Battle of Issus

In the following year, 333 BCE, the two armies met again near the town of Issus. Darius III had been surprised at the Macedonians' prior victory. This time, he took command of his army rather than rely on his satraps. His plan was to launch a surprise attack on the Macedonians, marching behind them as they advanced to Hellespontine and cutting off their supplies.

The Persians captured the town of Issus and marched as far as the Pinarus River when they saw Alexander's army approaching, forcing the Persians to set up camp there. The beginning of the battle seemed to go in the Persians' favor since the Macedonian army was unable to cross the river without being besieged.

Alexander the Great was finally able to break through the Persian forces in the center, with his right flank breaking through the Persian left flank, forcing the Persians to fall back. Alexander then charged directly for Darius III and his guard, forcing them to flee. Alexander may have given chase had he not seen his troops struggling and gone to their aid. When the Persians saw their king had fled, they, too, abandoned the battle. The Macedonians gave chase, resulting in the widespread massacre of the Persian army. This battle was a victory for the Macedonians and the definitive end of the Persian Empire. It was the first time the Persian army had ever lost with the king present.

Battle of Gaugamela

The loss at Issus led to the capture of Darius III's family. Darius III fled, leaving behind his family, and Alexander captured his wife, two daughters, and mother. Various messages pleading for their release reached Alexander, which he refused to do until Darius accepted him as the ruler of the Persian Empire. Alexander took over nearly all of southern Asia Minor with his last victory, while Darius III was forced to flee to Babylon and regroup.

Before waging another battle, Darius III attempted peaceful negotiations. Three attempts were made, with the final one offering Alexander his daughter's hand in marriage and joint rule of the Persian Empire. Alexander refused these offers and demanded that Darius either accept him as king or meet him in battle. Darius III began gathering his forces, encamping near Gaugamela. This news reached Alexander through some of the captive men from a fleeing Persian cavalry, most of whom managed to escape when faced with the Macedonians. With the knowledge of the Persians' whereabouts, Alexander headed for a final and decisive confrontation against the Persians in 331 BCE.

The Persian army is reported to have far outnumbered the Macedonians, and Alexander is credited with the use of superior military strategies. Knowing Darius III would not wish to attack first, citing the failure of that strategy at Issus, Alexander forced his hand with an unusual move, leaving Darius III vulnerable to an attack and making Darius come out into the open to fight. To deal with the issue of a much larger Persian force, the Macedonians used careful planning and reservation, allowing them to endure longer.

Alexander charged and weakened the center of the Persian army, leaving Darius III unguarded. Reports suggest that Darius, once again, abandoned his army and fled, with his army following suit. Alexander would have given chase if not for a message he received of his army struggling at the left flank, choosing to help them instead. Although the Persians put up a fierce fight, they fell.

The Last of the Achaemenid Dynasty: Darius III Falls

Darius managed to escape on horseback with a number of his cavalry. As he escaped, he gave a resounding speech about gathering another army to face and ultimately defeat Alexander and sent off messages to his satraps to remain loyal and stout. However, he may have counted too much on the loyalty of his people. Perhaps frustrated by the continuous losses or Darius III's cowardice, Darius's satrap, Bessus, who had fought alongside him, killed the Persian king.

Alexander the Great may be greatly respected for his military command and the empire he built, but he is also celebrated for his ethical stance during battles. When he found Darius III dead, he gave him a burial ceremony at Persepolis, the Persian capital, and hunted down Bessus. After the death of Darius III, the remaining satraps accepted Alexander as king and surrendered without war. Bessus later attempted to take the throne, calling himself Artaxerxes V and claiming to be the king of Persia. He was eventually captured, tortured, and killed by Alexander.

Darius III is regarded by many as inefficient, unsuitable for the throne, and cowardly. While unrest in Persia had been growing due to political instability, the empire still held on as it had before. However, during Darius III's reign, the whole of the Achaemenid Empire came to an end and was lost to foreign invaders. What is more, Darius's attempts at fighting the invaders were lackluster at best, as he abandoned his army more than once instead of engaging in battle to win or die nobly. With his death in 330 BCE, the Achaemenid dynasty officially came to an end.

PART FOUR:
ARTS, RELIGION, AND CULTURE

Chapter 12: Arts and Architecture

The Achaemenid Empire had much to boast about during its two-century rule. It grew to form the largest civilization of its time under the leadership of Cyrus the Great and his successors. The Achaemenid Empire added to its rapidly growing dynasty with its conquests, with various people groups and cultures assimilating under the Persian flag.

Their many conquests brought the Persian emperors untold riches, power, and influence that reached beyond the regions of their rule. As the empire grew, so did its art, design, architecture, and craftsmanship. In addition to leading conquests, many of the Persian emperors spent considerable wealth erecting beautiful examples of artistry and architecture that portray the skill and might of the Persians, some of which still exist to this day. While the Achaemenid Empire held great political influence, it also left behind a great cultural heritage.

History of Achaemenid Art

The Achaemenid Empire lasted a little over two centuries, from the mid-6th century to the mid-4th century BCE. In that time, it grew to become one of history's greatest empires, stretching from the Indus Valley in modern-day Pakistan to Egypt in the northeast corner of Africa. As the empire grew and expanded, it gained unsurmountable wealth, riches, and power. With that came the development of a unique culture, complete with its own language, history, and art.

Before the Persian Empire emerged, the region had been dominated by a number of other civilizations that brought their own culture, tradition, heritage, language, and art with them. A combination of influences ruled over ancient Persia, such as the Elamites, Assyrians, and Medes. When the Achaemenid Empire took control, it created a new culture derived from the influences of those who came before. Many of these dynasties had coexisted for some time in the Iranian Plateau, leading to a cultural mix that produced novel traditions.

The Achaemenid conquests also played a major role in the emerging art and architecture during this period. Some of the major influences came from the Greek, Babylonian, and Lydian cultures. Some Chinese influences can also be seen in Persian art; in particular, miniatures created as illustrations or independent artworks often featured Chinese characters. Roman, Mesopotamian, and Egyptian influences can also be seen in the Persian artwork produced during this time.

Persian architecture emerged as a synthesis of the various influences arising from the conquests and history of the empire. Its architectural prowess spanned from picturesque cities that served as centers of administration and governance and symbols of Achaemenid power to mausoleums and temples, which were designed to honor the fallen and worship the sacred gods revered by the people living in the Persian Empire. The previous Elamite, Assyrian, and Median civilizations, as well as the conquered lands of Egypt, Lydia, and Asia Minor, all contributed to the construction and design process adopted by the Persians. The result was something inherently unique and clearly identifiable as Persian craftsmanship.

Some of the most significant examples of Persian architecture that represent its style and influence are the royal tombs, such as those of Cyrus the Great and Artaxerxes IV. These tombs were a hallmark feature of the empire, as kings of the dynasty often built their own tombs. The city of Persepolis, which served as one of the empire's capitals, is another example of the Persian Empire's magnificence, as it served as the hub of governmental functions and ceremonial proceedings.

Two other important cities were Ecbatana and Susa, which remained the focus of many Persian emperors, with the rulers ordering the construction of various landmarks, which have stood the test of time and attest to the craft adopted by Persian builders and architects. The preserved structures in these cities offer a great insight into the development of Persian architecture, as it features construction carried out throughout the empire.

The Persians showed great skill in various facets of art and architecture. They are particularly known for their love and expertise in creating rock and frieze reliefs and their skill with precious metals. They used their reserves of gold and silver to create functional and decorative pieces. Columned halls are a distinctive feature of Persian architecture, appearing most significantly in the constructions of Xerxes I and Artaxerxes III.

Rock Reliefs

Carved rock reliefs could often be found on high points beside an important road or sources of water and were commonly used to mark a successful conquest. Rock reliefs first emerged in the Elamite civilization and were subsequently adopted by many later civilizations, including the Achaemenids, and were often carved in the same places. Under Persian emperors, such reliefs were typically used to boast of Persian power and illustrate the empire's might and extent. Some of the more significant examples include the Behistun Inscription and the Naqsh-e Rostam.

Behistun Inscription

Behistun Inscription.

The Behistun Inscription, which was written for Darius the Great, is a multilingual rock relief proclaiming the power of the Achaemenid dynasty. It first relates a short autobiography of Darius and continues to relate, in great detail, the rebellions that arose as a result of his predecessor's actions and Darius's success in suppressing them. The events are written in the Babylonian, Elamite, and Old Persian languages, and the inscription was crucial in helping to decipher the cuneiform script. As a proclamation of the empire's might, it also relates all the territories under Persian rule.

Naqsh-e Rostam

Naqsh-e Rostam.

The Naqsh-e Rostam serves as the tomb and final resting place for four Achaemenid kings near Persepolis. Various archaeological sites are carved into the face of the mountain besides the tombs, including the Ka'ba-ye Zartosht and the Sassanid reliefs, which date from the Elamite dynasty to the Sasanians. The tombs of the kings are cut into the cliff, as well as with various depictions, which include images of the kings being blessed by the gods and rows of other figures, presumably soldiers and the king's subjects, offering tribute.

The emperors' tombs are sometimes referred to as the Persian crosses based on the way they are structured. The entrance lies at the center of the cross, which leads into the chamber where the king lies in a sarcophagus. Of the four tombs found here, only the tomb of Darius I is explicitly labeled. The other three are believed to be those of Xerxes I, Artaxerxes I, and Darius II. A fifth unfinished tomb is also located here, which has been speculated to belong to either Artaxerxes IV or Darius

III; the latter's tomb has never been discovered to date. After the fall of the Achaemenid Empire, Alexander the Great's armies looted the tombs, along with many other Persian structures.

Frieze Relief

Frieze of Griffon, Palace of Darius.
Following Hadrian, CC BY-SA 2.0 <https://creativecommons.org/licenses/by-sa/2.0>, via Wikimedia Commons; https://commons.wikimedia.org/wiki/File:Frieze_of_Griffins,_circa_510_BC,_Apadana,_west_co urtyard_of_the_palace,_Susa,_Iran_Susa,_Iran,_Louvre_Museum_(12251831946).jpg

Frieze reliefs could be found in abundance in Persian architecture reliefs. These reliefs are sculptured decorative single panels portraying various designs. They are often found along royal staircases or buildings or as part of furniture. Many of these Achaemenid friezes can be found in Persepolis, particularly in palace architecture, such as in the throne rooms of Darius and Xerxes.

Most commonly, friezes appear in Achaemenid architecture as slabs with low carvings along staircases that lead to important ceremonial structures. Many of them feature or attempt to represent the empire's wealth by depicting servants bearing richly laden platters of drink and food for royal feasts.

One of the more recognizable frieze reliefs is the depiction of a Median. This relief is located along a stairway on the side of the Palace of Darius; however, it dates to the reign of Artaxerxes II. It portrays the Median, who can be identified by his dress, the typical tunic with a belt and a rounded cap, being led by a Persian. The frieze shows them walking hand in hand, perhaps representing harmonious relations following the conquest of the Medians.

Friezes that showcase the power of the Persian king are referred to as Treasure Reliefs, which illustrate scenes from across the empire, similar to the one found on the palace stairway. The Apadana in Persepolis features such scenes, such as one showing leaders and noblemen from the various Persian provinces appearing beneath a male lamassus, a design of a celestial being adopted from the Mesopotamian culture.

Paradise Gardens

One of the best depictions of Persian art and style is the gardens, which depict a particular Achaemenid influence. Known as the paradise gardens, they were typically designed in an enclosed, symmetrical style. A common and unique feature of these gardens was the *chahar bagh*, which literally translates to "four gardens," indicating the four-quarter split in the garden surrounding a body of water, usually a pond. Water and scents were essential elements of these gardens. Ponds, canals, and fountains were common features and were surrounded by fragrant flora.

The royal paradise garden at Pasargadae, which was built by Cyrus the Great, features the first known use of the *chahar bagh* design. A garden portico offers an opening through the garden, allowing not only an open landscape but also creating a fourfold design. This characteristic design is believed to be symbolic of the title Cyrus the Great held ("King of the Four Quarters of the World"). The garden is believed to have remained in use throughout the entirety of the Achaemenid Empire and is today designated as a World Heritage Site. It is one of the oldest remains of a Persian garden.

Precious Metalwork

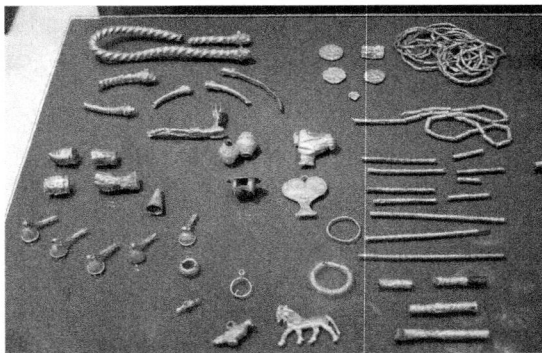

The Oxus Treasure.

The discovery of the Oxus Treasure in the 19th century supplemented the modern understanding of Persian skill with metalwork. The discovered treasure held about 180 pieces of precious metalwork, including about 200 coins, from the Achaemenid period. The original treasure may have held many more pieces, as some historical reports suggest treasures may have been lost or melted down over time.

The metalworking skill of the Persians is greatly evidenced in the discovered treasure. Persian craft was exemplary and advanced for its time. Many of these pieces display highly intricate designs, which reflect a similar theme to that found in carpet weaving, pottery, and reliefs of the time. The metalwork would often be inlaid with beautiful stones. The pieces found within the recovered treasure feature bracelets and armlets, which were common gifts and often presented to the emperor as tribute.

The Statue of Darius I

The statue of Darius I.

Among the sculptures and statues the Persians created, the most notable and often-occurring feature is the Taurus—a two-headed bull commonly found at the head of columns. Another example of their statue craftsmanship is the statue of Darius I, which was discovered in Susa. It is believed to have been made in Egypt, given the grey granite from which it is made that can be found in Egypt.

The statue features Darius I enrobed and armed with a dagger on his belt. Within the pleats of his robe can be seen inscriptions in cuneiform text, with the other side featuring hieroglyphs. It is believed Darius I may have commissioned this statue after the conquest of Egypt.

Persepolitan Columns

Persian architecture notably used columns. Their type of column design has its own distinct categorization and commonly features a strong base topped with double-sided animal heads, which would usually be bulls. Apadanas were enormous halls within Persian palaces that often featured hundreds of giant columns, such as those featured in the Hall of a Hundred Columns.

The stonework skill this type of architecture required did not exist in Persia but was found in neighboring regions and in many of the empires brought under Persian rule. The Achaemenid emperors had many territories at their disposal and were able to obtain the services of craftsmen from around the empire. This resulted in a crossbred architectural style, which boasted Egyptian, Mesopotamian, Lydian, and Elamite influences.

Hall of a Hundred Columns

Hall of a Hundred Columns.

The Hall of a Hundred Columns was started by Xerxes I but completed by his son and successor, Artaxerxes I. It features a northern entrance, with the portico decorated by two bulls—another hallmark of Persian architecture. Each of the one hundred columns features a wide base, which narrows as it proceeds to the top with a fluted shaft. The columns themselves are designed with floral patterns and topped by the signature two-headed bull. It functioned initially as a throne hall of Persepolis but may have become a storeroom later on to manage the vast treasures and wealth of the Achaemenid Empire.

The Royal Road

This ancient highway, which was refurbished by Darius I, served the purpose of improving communication links. It started in Sardis, crossing through Anatolia, Nineveh, and Babylonia, where it split; one end traveled through Ecbatana to what would become the Silk Road, and the other ran through Susa as far as Persepolis. Some parts of the road are believed to have been constructed during Assyrian rule, which Darius then improved and expanded.

It is believed the road was used up until the Roman period, with some parts of it, such as the bridge at Diyarbakir, still standing today. It stretched for over two thousand kilometers, and as a paved road, it could handle chariots and horse-drawn carts. Other than improving communication within the empire, the Royal Road also served to improve trade relations. As a military tool, it was particularly essential, enabling the Persian armies to cover great distances across the empire in comparatively shorter periods of time. It was a vastly important road to the empire and featured regular patrols and guard posts.

Chapter 13: Religion

Cyrus the Great's conquest of the Median Empire led to the establishment of the Achaemenid dynasty in 550 BCE. At the time of its formation, the empire was the largest ever seen and continues to be the largest empire in the history of the world based on the global population at the time. Forty-four percent of the world's population lived under the rule of the Achaemenid Empire.

Given such numbers, it stands to reason this was a diverse empire and included different nations, cultures, languages, and religions. To rule it successfully and for it to last as long as it did, an approach of acceptance and tolerance was needed, which was something its founder, Cyrus, championed.

Religious Policies of the Persian Empire

Religion played an important role within the Persian Empire. The Iranian Plateau had a rich religious history due to the many diverse groups of people that lived and conquered the land. By the time the Achaemenid Empire was born, many different religious traditions and affiliations already existed in Persia. Achaemenid conquests brought more religions under the rule of the empire.

The Cyrus Cylinder

The Cyrus Cylinder.
Prioryman, CC BY-SA 3.0 <https://creativecommons.org/licenses/by-sa/3.0>, via Wikimedia Commons; https://commons.wikimedia.org/wiki/File:Cyrus_Cylinder_front.jpg

After Cyrus the Great's conquest of Babylonia, he issued the Cyrus Cylinder, which narrates his conquest of Babylonia and the defeat of its king. It then goes on to detail his rules and policies for the regions under his rule. The Cyrus Cylinder promised religious freedom for members of all religious groups that were part of the Achaemenid Empire. Most notably, it granted Babylonian prisoners of war permission to return to their homelands. This act earned Cyrus praise for being a tolerant and just ruler.

Under his policies, Jewish prisoners of war who had been brought to Babylonia were able to return home to Jerusalem. Cyrus also granted them financial aid for their journey and political support, helping them rebuild their temple that had been destroyed in the war. Such acts of tolerance earned him great fame, and he set an example for his successors. Religious tolerance would become a hallmark of Achaemenid rule, at least until the years preceding its demise.

Magi

The Magi was the official designation of the priesthood that existed in the Median, Achaemenid, Parthian, and Sasanian Empires. During the latter two, the title Magi came to be referred to as Zoroastrian priests. The earliest designation of the Magi comes from among one of the six Median tribes, with one of them forming a priestly clan. Their position among the Medians was that of great influence and repute, as they acted as interpreters of dreams and fortune-tellers.

During the Elamite period, other priests hailing from local cults practiced and preached their beliefs. However, during the Median rule over Persia, the Magi came to hold greater significance, performing priestly functions on a much grander scale. Some of this influence may have carried on even after the fall of the Medians since the Magi continued to hold power during the Persian Empire.

Records during Darius I's reign show that the Magi acted as the official priests for the Achaemenid royalty and enjoyed great influence in the royal court. Other than religious responsibilities, the Magi were also involved in the administrative and economic spheres. In return for their services, they were supplemented from the royal stocks with flour, wine, beer, grain, rams, and fruit.

During the Achaemenid period, the Magi appeared in Babylonia and Egypt. This appearance was probably due to the empire's rule in these regions, with the Magi traveling there to perform some administrative functions. They also appear in Greek texts and are referred to during the battles fought between the Persians and the Greeks.

Xerxes I was known to make no major decision without advice from the Magi, who would also act as prophets and accompany the Persian army on campaigns. No sacrifices could be made without the presence of the Magi. Historical accounts suggest that the Magi held great influence within the Achaemenid court, and some were even appointed as guardians of the tomb of Cyrus the Great.

Some accounts, such as those of Herodotus, suggest no temples existed for Persian gods. However, a clearly defined religious hierarchy existed, designating the chief priest and the lesser priests. Little is known about the Persian religion and practice before the adoption of Zoroastrianism, as any religion before it existed primarily as an oral tradition with no written scripture.

Before the advent of Zoroastrianism, the Magi enjoyed great privilege and were the strongest opponents of the rise of Zoroastrianism. The social system and status quo benefitted them greatly, giving them status and wealth. The teachings of Zoroaster threatened to endanger this lifestyle for the Magi. After Zoroastrianism entered the region and was widely practiced in Persia, priests within the religion began to be referred to as Magi.

Zoroastrianism

The rise of Zoroastrianism began with Zoroaster or Zarathustra, a prophet of the religion who may have preached sometime between 1500 to 1000 BCE. Little is known of him except that he came from nobility and was part of the priestly class. Around the age of thirty, he is said to have received a revelation from a being of light called Vohu Manah, a representative of Ahura Mazda, the one true god. This being represented the goodness of thought, words, and deeds.

The revelation Zoroaster received at this time told him the current religious practices of the Magi were incorrect. Thus, Ahura Mazda was introduced to him as the true god, and Zoroaster was appointed his prophet. Because a priestly class already existed, Zoroaster's teachings were not immediately accepted. A particular class of the clergy, the Karpans, were particularly against everything Zoroaster had to say. This new religious teaching was perceived to be a threat to the status quo by the priestly class, which forced Zoroaster to renounce or flee.

Zoroaster traveled to King Vishtaspa, who is known as the first righteous king who accepted the faith as preached by Zoroaster. In Vishtaspa's court, Zoroaster debated the nature of divine truth with Vishtaspa's priests. Initially, Vishtaspa was not pleased with this challenge to his faith and had Zoroaster imprisoned. When Zoroaster was able to heal his paralyzed horse, the king released him and accepted the faith. With his influence, the Zoroastrian faith began to spread, replacing the polytheistic beliefs of the time.

Until his death at the age of seventy-seven, Zoroaster is believed to have continued his teachings, living a life of quiet devotion. While some accounts relate that he passed away of old age, others suggest that he may have been assassinated for his beliefs.

The Basis of Zoroastrianism

The Zoroastrian faith, which is still around today, follows five basic principles. These reflect the teachings of other monotheistic religions in that it preaches the existence of one supreme god. In Zoroastrianism, that god is Ahura Mazda. Just as Ahura Mazda is the embodiment of all that is good, his eternal nemesis, Angra Mainyu, is the embodiment of all that is evil. A man's goodness can be seen through his thoughts, words, and deeds, and each has the free will to choose good or evil for themselves.

Earlier gods and entities that had existed were reassigned as spiritual manifestations of Ahura Mazda. Preexisting concepts became assimilated into this new faith, including that of Chinvat Bridge, which describes death as the crossing of a dark river via boat, the Crossing of the Separator. In Zoroastrianism, this bridge reflects the deeds of the person attempting to cross it, becoming narrow and razor-sharp for the condemned and becoming wider and easier to cross for the righteous. Two guards overseeing the bridge welcome the righteous while snarling at the condemned souls. The angel Suroosh guides and guards the souls as they cross, and the maiden of the bridge, Daena, comforts the souls as they come to the crossing.

Zoroastrianism largely operates on the principle of good and evil. There are both benevolent and malevolent spirits to be found roaming the world called the ahuras and the daevas, respectively. Since their influence exists all around the world and since humans have the free will to choose what they follow, it is an individual's responsibility to guard themselves against the evil and negative and accept the righteous and positive. In the same way, it is an individual's responsibility to lead a life of honesty, truthfulness, and honor, rejecting lies and deception. By doing so, one can enter paradise after death.

However, failure to lead a righteous life did not result in eternal punishment in the House of Lies. In Zoroastrianism, a savior-like figure, Saoshyant, will bring the End of Time when all souls will be forgiven and reunite with their creator. Angra Mainyu will be defeated once and for all, and everyone, whether righteous or condemned, will live in eternal bliss.

Ahura Mazda

Ahura Mazda.
A. Davey, CC BY 2.0 <https://creativecommons.org/licenses/by/2.0>, via Wikimedia Commons; https://commons.wikimedia.org/wiki/File:Ahura_Mazda.jpg

The all-good, all-powerful creator of life, Ahura Mazda, is believed to have birthed the other, lesser gods. He embodies all the positive, bright forces, which clash with the negative, dark forces intent on creating chaos through Angra Mainyu. The world, as created by Ahura Mazda, came to be in seven steps, beginning with the sky or, according to other traditions, water. This world would have brought about universal harmony were it not for the devious actions of Angra Mainyu.

The sky came to be in the form of an orb that held water, and the different bodies of water were separated by the earth, which was granted vegetation to sustain life. Ahura Mazda then went on to create the primordial bull, Gavaevodata, which was killed by Angra Mainyu. His corpse was carried to the moon, where it was purified. All other animals were born through Gavaevodata.

This concept of Ahura Mazda's creations, which were later destroyed or corrupted by Angra Mainyu, exists throughout the Zoroastrian faith. When the first human, Gayomart, was created, Angra Mainyu killed him because of his beauty. The man's seed was purified in the sun, birthing a rhubarb plant from which manifested the first couple on earth, Mashya and Mashyana. Ahura Mazda granted them souls, and they were to live in peace and harmony with one another. However, they were corrupted by Angra Mainyu, who convinced them of Ahura Mazda's treachery as a false god. The couple fell from grace and were banished to live in a world of chaos and strife.

Although the couple was forced into a world of conflict, they could still choose to live a life of truth and honesty, repenting to Ahura Mazda and rejecting the influence of Angra Mainyu. Thus, the essence of this faith was the battle between good and evil. All other entities within the faith, including supernatural beings, fall on either end of the spectrum, with humans also forced to make a choice between the two sides.

Zoroastrianism underwent many modifications, particularly after the death of Zoroaster. For example, the crossing of the bridge was altered to include a final judgment when a soul's deeds would be balanced against each other. The souls that led a life of truth would be admitted to the House of Song, their final paradise. Naysayers would go into the darkness and confusion, finding their ultimate end in the House of Lies, which was similar to the Christian hell.

Human Life under Zoroastrianism

The beginning of human life was intended as a gift, as the soul Ahura Mazda had given them was supposed to be cherished and cared for. Ahura Mazda took care of the humans' needs and only asked that they care for their souls by adhering to his teachings and acting as defenders of his values, namely truth, honesty, and righteousness. Human life gained its meaning from the protection of the gift it had been granted. However, the meaning was lost by rejecting that gift, instead following Angra Mainyu's vengeful purpose.

While humans had free will to choose the path they would take in life, Ahura Mazda intended to guide them to the right path. For this purpose, he created a legion of lesser beings who would aid people in making the right choices and protect them from the dark forces of Angra Mainyu. These included Mithra, the god of the rising sun, Hvar Ksata, the god of the full sun, and Ardvi Sura, the goddess of health and fertility.

Worship rituals in Zoroastrianism center around the four elements, as that is how Ahura Mazda created the world in the beginning. It begins with fire, which is lit on the outer altar, and ends with water, which celebrates the elements of life, as it stands on earth and is surrounded by air. Of these elements, fire is the most important, but all elements are respected and sacred.

The Persian religion did not feature temples or statues because of a basic Zoroastrian tenet that their god was everywhere. The idea of a single building that could contain their god was unacceptable, as it was believed impossible and inappropriate. The use of the four elements in their worship made other regions, like the Greeks, report that the Persians worshiped fire. This was inaccurate, as the Persians used the elements to symbolize their god and worshipped their divine power alone.

Zoroastrianism in the Achaemenid Empire

Zoroastrianism was one of the major religions practiced in the Iranian Plateau, and much evidence indicates that the Achaemenid Empire's rulers observed the religion. Following Cyrus the Great's many conquests that led to the establishment of the Achaemenid dynasty, he is known to have praised Ahura Mazda for his success. While this led to the assumption that he was a Zoroastrian, other sources suggest this may not be entirely true.

Historical records show Ahura Mazda as an entity that may have predated the advent of Zoroastrianism. He was considered the supreme deity, and Cyrus's worship of the god does not necessarily indicate affiliation with Zoroastrianism. Similarly, there is no concrete proof of the religious inclination of later emperors, although most sources suggest they practiced Zoroastrianism. Ahura Mazda, in particular, is praised in various artwork, decrees, and Darius I's Behistun Inscription.

The Achaemenid Empire's policy of religious tolerance meant that the religion practiced by the royal house was never imposed on its subjects. This is also the reason it is difficult to determine with absolute certainty which religion was practiced by the Persian nobility. However, this religious independence is believed to have birthed Zurvanism. This movement stemmed from Zoroastrianism. The supreme deity in Zurvanism was Zurvan, or Time, who created Ahura Mazda and Angra Mainyu. The two were created as equals and locked in a cosmic struggle, whose ultimate victor would be Ahura Mazda. Zurvanism thought is believed to have gained traction during the second half of the Achaemenid Empire but did not become relevant on a larger scale until much later during the Sasanian period.

Chapter 14: Military

The force of the Persian military is attested to by the might of the Achaemenid Empire. Since most of the empire's conquests were preceded by war, the Persian military can be credited with expanding the Persian Empire.

Whether the true credit of the military's victories can be attributed to the strength of the military, its skill, or its leadership is hard to say; however, its contribution to the empire is undeniable. Over the course of Achaemenid rule, the Persian military expanded and grew to include greater numbers and superior weaponry. Even at the time of the Persian military's final defeat at the hands of Alexander the Great, it greatly outnumbered its opponent.

Distribution of the Persian Military

The Persian military consisted of five main divisions, with tactics based on the movement of these groups. They included the archers, the cavalry, the infantry, the chariots, and later the war fleet.

Archers

Persian archers.

The Persian archers were held in high regard since they were stationed on the front lines. The Persian tactic was to have the *sparabara,* or the shield-bearers, form a defensive line at the head of the army. The archers would then mount an attack on the opposing force, firing over the shield-bearers. This would pave the way for the infantry and cavalry to launch a more vicious attack against a now-exhausted opponent. The bow was also the national arm of the Achaemenid Empire, indicating the importance of archers in the military.

Scythian archers were hired by the Persians to train their archers since they had superior abilities. For this reason, the Scythians greatly influenced Persian archers, including their fighting style and weaponry. The Persians also adopted the Scythian bow and altered the bow to be recurved and made of wood rather than a chord, which granted greater flexibility when the arrow was released. Their arrows were also modified to be lighter and featured a bronze tip.

The altered bow and arrow proved so light and useful to carry that even infantrymen carried a bow and some arrows onto the battlefield. The Persian innovations, combined with their military tactics, led to the archers being considered some of the most superior military fighters of their time, even more so than the elite Cretans, the Greek archers. Persian archers played a key role in the success of the Persian military during expansionist conquests.

Cavalry

Cyrus the Great first realized the importance of the cavalry after watching the Greek military, which utilized cavalry units to great advantage. Taking inspiration from the Khorasan horseman, Cyrus organized the Persian cavalry to form the world's greatest mounted army at the time. The light cavalry carried altered Scythian bows. The light cavalry was made up of diverse nationalities and instigated battles by drawing an opponent into the fight.

The heavy cavalry, on the other hand, featured mostly Persian men who were armed with the usual weaponry of the infantry: battle axes, shields, and bows. Later on, this weaponry was updated, and the cavalrymen would carry javelins, which had a feared reputation among Persian enemies. The cavalry also carried long wooden or metal lances, shields, and spears.

Chariots

Chariots were not limited to a military designation during the Achaemenid Empire; they also served a ceremonial purpose and were used as command vehicles. The Persian emperors, particularly Xerxes I, were known to ride into battle in chariots. A special, empty chariot would also make an appearance. It was dedicated to Ahura Mazda and was pulled by eight white horses, giving him a place to join the Persians in battle.

The Persian scythed chariots remained one of their most deadly and effective innovations. Cyrus the Great, who had never seen much utility in the chariot as a military weapon, commissioned the scythed chariot, which was a far more effective weapon. It operated like a regular chariot but had swords attached to the wheels, which stuck out on either side. The swords could sever or seriously damage the limbs of their victims.

The scythed chariot became a vicious weapon for the Persians, who inflicted great damage on their enemy without much danger to themselves. Its original purpose was to breach the Greek defensive lines. Their heavy infantry formation had proven too strong for the Persian cavalry, but the scythed chariots made it an easy task.

Persian Fleet

The Persian fleet was largely adopted from the Greek triremes and biremes. The fleet featured long, narrow ships. The triremes had three levels of rowers with a long oar in the back. In the front, an iron beam ram was set, which was designed to stab and attack opponent ships and potentially destroy them. The biremes supported only two levels of rowers and carried two hundred men rather than three hundred. It otherwise performed many of the same functions as the trireme.

The Persian navy did not exist at the beginning of the Achaemenid Empire; it was launched by Cambyses II for the Battle of Pelusium against Egypt. Darius I used the navy for the conquest of lands in Asia Minor to face the Greek navy. With their navy, the Persians were able to conquer Thrace and Samos and fought against the Scythians.

The Persian navy is believed to have been led by commanders chosen from the imperial aristocracy. Many of these commanders may have been non-Persian since the Persians did not originally hold a fleet and therefore had no experience in commanding one. These early commanders may have been Carians, although some were also reported to be Greek. Little is known about sailors of lower rank other than that Phoenician rowers and sailors were hired at some point. The marines were made up almost entirely of Medians, Persians, and Scythians.

The Persian navy had a profound impact on the future of naval warfare in the region. They formed what would be the first true imperial navy, as they established the first trireme navy in history. The navy also laid the basis for Iranian naval engineering that would come later. The naval bases enjoyed great benefits due to their position, and the regions they were located in enjoyed great wealth.

The Diversity of the Persian Military

The Persian Empire assimilated various regions under its rule, and with that came the recruitment of military personnel from a variety of regions. As a result, the Persian army was one of the most diverse at the time.

Historical records suggest that a nation's contribution of soldiers to the Persian army came from its proximity to Persia. In lieu of paying tribute to the empire, nations could contribute more soldiers to the army. As a result, the Medians contributed the largest number of soldiers and imperial generals. The remainder of the army was made up of

Scythians, Egyptians, Ethiopians, Indians, Bactrians, and other groups.

The incorporation of these various groups into the Persian army also introduced different military techniques and weaponry. The archery bows from the Scythians, the triremes from the Greeks, and the war elephants from the Indians soon became a common sight on Persian battlefields. The Persians also came to rely heavily on mercenaries, particularly toward the end of Cyrus the Great's reign and during the rule of Cambyses II.

Greek mercenaries were very useful for the Persian army. For one, the Persian weaponry and armor were deemed to be inferior to that of the Greeks. Mercenaries were loyal to their employers and possessed skills and knowledge of tactics not known to the Persians. Since mercenaries were committed to war, they could fight with a zeal not found among other soldiers in the army. Mercenaries were sometimes even hired as generals and became part of the king's personal guard.

Division and Tactics of the Persian Army

The Persian army is believed to have amounted to roughly between 120,000 to 150,000 men, excluding the military support they gained from their allies. The *hazarabam*, which was made up of a thousand troops, was considered the best of the Persian regiments. Ten *hazarabams* made up the elite unit called the Immortals. They were the king's personal guards and were highly trained.

The default Persian war tactic was to use shields, through *sparabaras*, along the front lines and have archers launch the attack. The Persian army was also trained in shock tactics, which involved hand-to-hand combat, though this was not the Persians' preferred move, as they favored maintaining their distance from the opponent and defeating them through missile-style attacks.

The attack would typically begin with the actions of the light cavalry, who would seek to instigate the enemy. These were small attacks, with the soldiers using arrows and small javelins to goad their opponent to attack as the archers prepared an offensive. The cavalry would then move to attack the flanks, causing the opponent to gather together in a dense formation, which would make it difficult to maneuver. If the army chose to disperse instead, it would be subjected to shock attacks. In this way, Persian opponents, even the Greeks, suffered heavy casualties on the battlefield.

The Persian tactic was effective in theory but did not always work. For it to be effective, the Persians required large, open terrain that would not hinder the quick movements of the cavalry. It also required good timing and coordination between the cavalry, the archers, and the infantry and the inferiority of their opponent's weaponry and limited mobility. When the Persian army suffered a defeat, it was for the lack of one or more of these requirements.

For example, the Scythians engaged in scorched-earth tactics. They remained highly mobile and never engaged long enough with the Persian army to allow it to deploy its war tactics. This led to the Persians giving chase to the Scythians in a land wholly unfamiliar to them while the Scythians destroyed all possible resources, leaving nothing behind for the Persians to use.

The Battle of Marathon against the Greeks also resulted in failure for the Persians. The battle was conducted on a rocky slope, which was unfit for the Persians to scale and launch an attack. The Athenians returned to the plain when the Persians retreated to their ships, so the Athenians were able to avoid the hail of Persian arrows to engage them in close-quarters combat. The Athenians had no issues with mobility and did not have inferior weapons or skills the Persians could exploit. And although Alexander the Great's army was inferior in number, it was able to defeat the Persian forces due to superior tactical planning and the diverse divisions of Alexander's army. It comprised a variety of cavalry and infantry units that could launch attacks on all types of terrain with a variety of weaponry, forcing the Persians into close combat, where they were greatly outclassed.

The Greeks had far superior armor, which deflected the arrows and small javelins launched as part of the Persians' initial attack. Once the Persians had been forced into close combat, they stood little chance of victory since their inferior weaponry and lack of armor could not compete with the Greeks, though they did not possess any less valor or spirit than their opponents. The Persian army also relied heavily on their leader or king in battle. Although they remained coordinated under his guidance, they would immediately fall into disarray if the military leader was called or forced to flee, as was the case when Darius III faced off against the forces of Alexander the Great.

Preparing for Battle

While the Persian army had great strength in numbers, it was rarely sufficient for large expeditions. In such cases, the army needed to be recruited, and the process could take years. The Persian Empire held garrisons in important city centers, and the satraps had their own guard and local army. However, these were not called on to launch a campaign since it would leave the satrap vulnerable and defenseless in the face of a potential rebellion.

Mercenaries and tribal warriors were much easier to recruit and gather in times of need. They would be summoned to the *handaisa*, the recruiting stations, where they would be reviewed and recruited. The army would store provisions along the route it took for the campaign, although the men also carried supplies in baggage carts. Given the importance of religion in Persian culture, the Magi would accompany such campaigns, chanting hymns while circling the commander. They would carry an eagle standard and holy fire in portable holders.

Scouts would be sent ahead to watch for the enemy's movements. The military also established a great and reliable communication system while on the move. The Royal Road served as a way for couriers to convey messages quickly. The couriers would maintain their speed by changing horses frequently. The Persians also used fire signals to send news quickly.

The Persian army largely relied on day marches, as commanders disliked advancing or attacking at nighttime. The daytime procession was slow, owing to the baggage they often carried. In addition to provisions for the journey and the war, the procession would often include litters for the king's and commanders' wives and concubines. At nighttime, the army would make encampments on flat areas. If they feared an enemy approach, they would dig ditches, setting up sandbag defenses around them. Before the beginning of a battle, a council was held to discuss strategies and tactics.

Chapter 15: Languages and the Truth Issue

The Persian Empire adopted the Persian language, also known as Parsi, which remained the predominant language throughout the Achaemenid rule. Persian is part of the Indo-Iranian language group, and the spread and use of the language reached from Indian borders to Egypt and the Mediterranean and may have also influenced regions in the north. Old Persian, known locally as *ariya*, appears in the records and inscriptions from the Achaemenid period, most notably on Darius I's Behistun Inscription.

In modern times, the Parsi language has changed its form and is spoken and written beyond the regions of the Middle East. The Achaemenid Empire carried the Persian language with them into the subcontinent of India with their conquest of the Indus Valley. It remained a popular language in the royal courts until the arrival of the British, who banned many local languages.

Old Persian

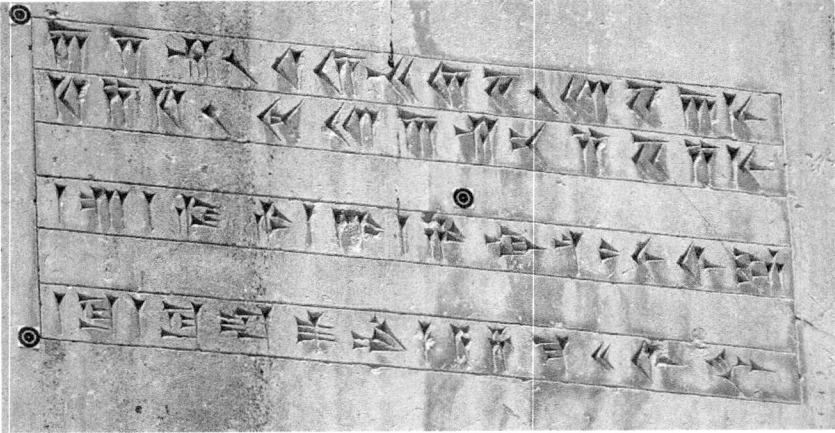

Old Persian inscription in Persepolis.

Old Persian is largely regarded as the language of the Achaemenid Empire. The language is used in administrative and legal texts and inscriptions celebrating the life and conquests of the Persian emperors. Its oldest recorded use is the Behistun Inscription, although the language dates back much further. A tribe by the name of Parsuwash is thought to have brought the language with them into the Iranian Plateau early in the 1st millennium BCE.

Later Assyrian records indicate the use of ancient Iranian languages, including the Persian and Median languages. Old Persian features many words from the Median language, which is now extinct, indicating its usage in the region long before the Achaemenid Empire came to be. The Behistun Inscription does not limit itself to one language. It repeats the same text in three cuneiform script languages: Old Persian, Elamite, and Babylonian. This indicates that, just as with religion, language diversity was welcome in the Persian Empire.

Even during the Achaemenid Empire, Old Persian did not retain its original form and developed and morphed into what is now known as the post-Old Persian language or pre-Middle Persian, as it lies in between the two distinct formations of the language. The language is evident in the 4th century BCE, where the inscriptions of Darius I differ greatly from the later inscriptions made during Artaxerxes II's and Artaxerxes III's reigns.

This form of Old Persian acted as a bridge to the Middle Persian language, which further evolved into New Persian. With each successive morphing, the language and syntax became more simplistic and straightforward than the one before it.

Middle Persian

The Middle Persian language gained traction after the Achaemenid Empire during the Sasanian period. Other than inscriptions and a few unearthed records during the Achaemenid Empire, few examples can be found of their writings, so we don't know the extent and diversity of the languages used during this time. However, many written texts, especially of the religious variety, have been unearthed from the Sasanian period that indicate the shift from Old Persian to Middle Persian.

The development of Middle Persian, like other Middle Iranian languages, began sometime in the mid-5th century BCE and continued until the 7th century CE. This period of development is marked by a change in the way the language was spoken, written, and used. The language was influenced by the empire's changes as well, taking on many features from the Greek language. Old Persian, as had been used by the Achaemenids, featured the Aramaic language, which began to lose its influence over time.

Modern Persian

Modern Persian, New Persian, or Farsi evolved from Middle Persian and is not wholly of Iranian origin. The language was slow to change, and the metamorphosis took until the 10th or 11th century CE and eventually formulated into the version known today. It took great influence from a variety of languages, including English, French, and German, but the most notable contribution comes from the Arabic language, which replaced many of the original Persian terms.

While European words exist in the Persian language, be it English or French, they exist largely out of necessity. Words for terms like "car" simply did not exist in the Persian language, and the solution was to import the word rather than invent a suitable term. Other words, like *merci*, which have suitable Persian counterparts, simply became enmeshed into the language to the degree that they sound natural rather than foreign to its speakers.

However, Arabic influence on the language was different. Not only did it replace the original Persian script, but many Arabic words and terms also outright replaced Persian words. This evolution of the Persian language is considered harmful since it completely annihilated many parts of the Persian language. These parts of the language are now extinct and sound more foreign to Persian speakers than the non-Persian words of their language.

The Use of Language in the Achaemenid Culture

Old Persian did not become one of the Achaemenid languages until much later. Starting with the reign of Cyrus the Great up until the rule of Darius I, the center of the Persian Empire was at Susa in Elam. Given this, the primary language of the administration remained Elamite since it made the most sense. The use of Elamite is attested in the tablets and fortifications found at Persepolis.

However, while Elamite remained the official language, it was not the only language used, even in the early days of the Achaemenid Empire. Any use of Elamite was always accompanied by text written in Old Persian, Babylonian, or Akkadian. This multilingual approach has led historians to believe that Elamite may have served as the central language in Susa. In other regions of the empire, other languages may have taken precedence. In any case, after the mid-5th century BCE, there is no recorded use of Elamite in Achaemenid-era records.

The Persians and Aramaic

Following Cyrus the Great's conquest of Mesopotamia, Aramaic was introduced to the Achaemenid Empire. Originating in Mesopotamia, it is believed to have been adopted by the Persians as their official language, which would help govern the diverse regions under Persian rule that otherwise hosted vastly different languages, peoples, and cultures. While many believe the Persians used Aramaic as an official language, there is no official document or inscription suggesting it was ever adopted as such. In fact, no such claim exists for any language used during the Achaemenid Empire. Aramaic was more pervasively used within the Persian Empire, and it continued to survive long after the demise of the Achaemenid.

The use of Old Persian was equally widespread; however, based on the recovered seals, artistic objects, and inscriptions, it may have been more commonly used in the western regions of Iran. The evolution of the language was rather drastic and differed greatly from its original form by the start of Artaxerxes II's reign. The reason behind this is believed to be that the language, in its original form, had largely been forgotten by that time in favor of other languages used within the empire. The scribes who wrote texts in Old Persian attempted to do so by recreating older inscriptions, obtaining imperfect and barely accurate results.

Greek Influence

The Achaemenids' entanglement with the Greeks meant that they did, at least occasionally, conduct some correspondence in the Greek language. The Persians had extensive, if usually hostile, relations with the Greeks, and they also conquered many Greek regions in Asia Minor. In addition, Greek mercenaries were a major part of the Persian army, and the Persians often forged alliances with the Greeks to aid in various campaigns. Artaxerxes II also acted as an arbiter to initiate the King's Peace between various Greek city-states. Therefore, the Greek language played an important role in the Persian bureaucracy.

However, there are no written records of Greek linguistic influences on the Achaemenid Empire. In addition to the Persians' frequent dealings with the Greeks, there is evidence to indicate that many Greeks also lived within the Achaemenid Empire, especially within Iran. Greek builders were involved in the construction of various Persian monuments, and some Greek inscriptions have been discovered at Persepolis. It seems inevitable that the Achaemenid Empire used, to some extent, the Greek language within its administrative circle.

Communication in the Persian Empire

One of the tenets of a successful empire is its communication channels. To run an empire as vast and diverse as the Achaemenid Empire, effective and quick communication was a prerequisite. Without it, not only would administrative processes come to a halt, but the empire would also be ill-equipped to respond to sudden threats. So, messages needed to be sent out quickly and reliably, but they also had to be relayed in a language that could be understood by all.

Hierarchy of Communication

Communication within the Achaemenid Empire followed a top-down route, starting at the royal court. Directives and orders were issued by the king, which were then passed to the satraps. These satraps would then carry out these directives in their respective regions of governance. The deployment of satraps to regional courts was intended to be an extension of the king's court, where his accepted practices were to be emulated.

This also established a more effective channel of communication. The Achaemenid Empire held a vast geographical region under its rule; attempting to disperse any message effectively throughout the kingdom would be a great challenge. Since the satraps were usually members of the royal family, they could be relied on to uphold royal tradition at regional courts and to maintain efficient and swift communication channels throughout their respective regions.

Correspondence

Since Aramaic had been adopted following the Mesopotamian conquest and established as the administrative language, it widely served as the major language of correspondence. The multilingual nature of the Achaemenid Empire necessitated this practice since there was no other way to ensure communication between the various satrapies. There is no record of the Achaemenid emperors themselves showing a preference for any particular language.

With a single administrative language, the work of scribes was made easier since they had only to learn Aramaic to fulfill their role in the royal court. Very few examples of royal correspondence survive, as much of it was inscribed on perishable items. The few surviving samples of communication between various satraps form the belief that Aramaic was largely relied on as the official language of communication.

The Truth Issue

One of the central tenets of Persian life, which is noted by various historians, is the focus on truthfulness. This is largely believed to have stemmed from a religious perspective. Zoroastrianism, one of the most commonly practiced religions in the Persian Empire, portrays Ahura Mazda as an all-powerful god, a being of light that values truth and honesty. Following his practices and upholding these principles was what gave meaning to life. It stands to reason then that the truth was very important in Persian life. Based on historical accounts, nothing was more disgraceful than telling a lie, and this would influence many Persian policies and practices.

However, it may be inaccurate to say that the importance of truth emerged from a religious basis. Even before the spread of Zoroastrianism, the Persian people followed a basic set of ethics that defined their lives. In the absence of orderly courts, laws, and enforcers of any such policies, a code of honor ruled supreme among the various Iranian tribes, among which was the basic tenet of truth-telling. Even those who had not grown up within the teachings of any religion followed and valued such ethical principles, forming a core part of Persian life.

Lying was considered the basis of every evil in Persian morality, within and outside the practice of Zoroastrianism. The Zoroastrian book, the Avesta, also mentions the fallacy of lying, stating that it led to the corruption of the righteous man. The concept of truth-telling was so deeply entrenched in Persian thought that Darius I used it to justify his actions to take the throne.

The Behistun Inscription narrates Darius I's ascension to the throne and the actions he then took to suppress rebellions in the Persian Empire. The inscription lists the names of a series of deceivers, including the imposter Bardiya, whose lies and deceit caused the nation to fall into rebellion, leading to unrest, chaos, and strife. Darius I emerged from this havoc as the bearer of light and truth, having quashed the rebellion and dealt with the challengers of Ahura Mazda.

Chapter 16: Government of the Empire

When Cyrus the Great founded the Achaemenid Empire, he established an organized regime. The empire boasted four capital cities during Cyrus's reign, which served as hubs for the administrative management of the vast, multi-regional empire. These four cities were Pasargadae, Susa, Ecbatana, and Babylon. These cities were also intended to show off the might and power of the Persian Empire.

The Achaemenid Empire also established a somewhat regional manner of governance. The satrapy system established administrative units across the empire, where governors or satraps were installed to oversee the region. In addition to the satrap, a general was also employed to manage military operations, and there was a state secretary for record-keeping. As the empire grew, so did the satrapies, and the Achaemenid form of governance influenced many later regimes.

The System of Governance

The satrapy system was not new to the Iranian Plateau, as it had been implemented by the Medians and the Assyrians before them. Cyrus drew inspiration for his own government from them, though he chose to make some vital changes. The Persian Empire is believed to have taken the greatest influence from foreign empires than any empire before it.

A common aspect of the Persian Empire and those that preceded it was that they all ruled over a diverse group of people. However, unlike the Persian Empire, the previous dynasties had neither been as large nor harmonious in their rule and so disintegrated. Cyrus the Great learned this lesson from the Assyrians and Medians, and it was a mistake he did not wish to repeat. One of the policies he wished to avoid was the Assyrian practice of the forced removal and deportation of large groups.

This forced relocation was not wholly insensitive; families were never separated, and people were transported based on where their skills may be needed most. Regardless, the forced move did not foster any goodwill for the ruling power. Previous empires also made no effort to preserve the cultures of their conquered lands. People belonging to regions were stripped of their identity instead of being embraced as new regions of the empire. Religious practices of the conquered lands were also ignored in favor of establishing the religious preference of the ruling empire.

While the official religion of the Achaemenid court is still debated, it is well known that no religion, cultural ideology, or tradition was imposed upon conquered subjects. People were free to practice whatever faith they chose, speak whichever languages they preferred, and continue living their lives as they had before. Cyrus the Great's liberation of the Jews from Babylonia is seen as another example of his commitment to this approach of acceptance and the mark of a true leader. The only obligation placed on newly acquired lands was that they pay their share of taxes and contribute men to the army.

While regional governments existed in the Achaemenid Empire, they were not entirely independent. In particular, during the rule of Cyrus the Great, officials were employed to keep an eye on the satraps. They would report regional affairs back to the king, acting as his "eyes and ears." This practice may have contributed, at least in part, to the peace the empire experienced during this time, for there is no record of any revolts during Cyrus's reign.

Achaemenid policies regarding tolerance for crime or treachery differed based on the emperors. Cyrus's successor, his son Cambyses, is often believed to have been harsher in the punishments he exacted as a ruler and thus seen as unfit for the throne. While he conquered Egypt, he also forged hostilities with the Egyptians and the Greeks, which might explain his more severe approach.

Ordinance of Good Regulations

Cambyses's successor, Darius I, took a more liberal approach, instituting what he called the Ordinance of Good Regulations. Given the lack of written records of the time, there is little known about the details of the ordinance. However, one of its essential principles related to the punishments for crimes, urging everyone, even the king, to reconsider harsh punishments for a crime. Rather, a person's good deeds should be taken into consideration when making any judgment.

Darius chose lenient punishments for first-time offenses, particularly when weighed against the individual's services. For instance, a judge who was caught taking a bribe would not be crucified, a punishment Cambyses would have thought just. Instead, Darius would have demoted the judge if that was his only offense.

The organization of the empire received further attention during this period, as Darius divided the kingdom into seven regions. These regions were further divided into twenty satrapies. Following Cyrus's policy of maintaining watch over the empire, Darius instituted a similar system. A royal treasurer was hired to ensure the satraps' spending and activities happened with the king's approval. In addition, inspectors were recruited whose job was to check up on various satraps. They would keep an eye on government officials, ensuring all jobs were being performed honestly. Another committee was tasked with reviewing revenue collection from each satrap, ensuring all citizens were registered, all taxes were being fairly imposed and paid, and that they were all being routed where they should. This may be considered a just and fair system designed to prevent corruption and protect the rights of all.

Chapar Khaneh

The postal system was not a new invention. The Neo-Assyrians and the Neo-Babylonians had already been using some type of mail delivery system. However, the Achaemenids' innovation created what can be referred to as the closest predecessor to the modern mailing system. The Royal Road played a pivotal role, as it connected various far-flung regions of the empire, cutting long journeys into a matter of days.

Messages would be delivered by horse-riding couriers through a relay system that allowed the speedy and consistent delivery of letters and messages. The Iranians, including during the Persian Empire, were particularly adept at horseback riding, and their delivery system involved changing horses at frequent intervals to ensure consistent speed. Since all administrative correspondence was done in Aramaic, it ensured a standardized language, which also aided the speed of delivery. The Chapar Khaneh, or postal service station, was located at intervals along the Royal Road.

The Taxation System

While an earlier taxation model was established by Cyrus, Darius I is believed to have improved on it, creating a just, fair, and well-distributed setup. Taxation was decided based on the economic capability of each satrapy, such as their productivity and how much each could realistically contribute. Based on their individual strengths—for instance, Egypt for its crops —each satrapy was required to pay that substance in taxation. Babylon is believed to have the greatest economic potential and consequently paid the greatest amount in taxes.

The Persians were not subject to the taxation system. It was reserved strictly for conquered lands, which could also contribute more soldiers to the empire's army in place of paying higher taxes.

Slavery was not a very common practice in the Persian Empire, but it did happen. Slavery had existed in the region before the Achaemenid Empire, and the term used to describe them, *bandaka*, referred to general dependence. The term slavery was often used to denote the kingly status of the emperor, marking the public as his subjects, making the degree of the practice of slavery during the Persian Empire unclear. Enslavement is also mentioned in regard to the conquest of neighboring lands that became part of the Persian Empire. Future empires that succeeded the Achaemenids would derive inspiration from this system to establish their own administrative policies.

Achaemenid Coinage

Achaemenid coinage.
Classical Numismatic Group, Inc. http://www.cngcoins.com, CC BY-SA 3.0
<http://creativecommons.org/licenses/by-sa/3.0/>, via Wikimedia Commons;
https://commons.wikimedia.org/wiki/File:Cyprus_and_Achaemenid_Archer_design.jpg

The use of coinage, in particular gold coin, was first attributed to the Lydians around the mid-6th century BCE. Lydia was conquered by Cyrus, and the coinage system was introduced on a much wider scale throughout the Persian Empire.

Before the conquest of Lydia, the coinage system was a foreign concept to the Persians. The barter system was the basis of economic activity, with some use of silver bullion. The coinage system brought about an economic revolution; Lydia had already been a leading power in trade through its invention.

Sardis became an important city center. The mint was located there, so Sardis acted as a capital city for the western Achaemenid region. Coinage coming out of Sardis supplied this region, becoming a vital force in making the Achaemenid Empire economically strong. When Darius I became king, he revolutionized the existing coinage system by minting it with images of Persepolis. The term for the gold coin, the daric, is even believed by some to have been derived from his name, Darius I, either because of his influence on the coinage system or the belief that he introduced the system in Persia.

The original Lydian coins were designed by a system of incuse punches on one side and some pictorial design on the other. Darius I simplified the Lydian model, which used two punches, replacing it with one. Earlier pictorial designs were adopted from the Lydians, which included animal designs and geometric shapes. Other than pictures of Persepolis, the Persians also used images of archers, which represented the might of the Achaemenid military.

Transportation

The trading system set up under the Achaemenid rule was supplemented by extensive infrastructure and a reliable coinage system. Tariffs earned from trade were a lucrative source of income for the empire, which also included agricultural and tribute taxes. The Persian economy, particularly after the introduction of Lydian coinage, was greatly boosted. However, its greatest support came from the infrastructure that the emperors, in particular Cyrus and Darius I, invested to boost trade efficiency and revenue.

The Royal Road provided various stations and caravanserais, or roadside inns, for merchants and couriers alike, helping to create a trading system that was like no other at the time. Trade along the Royal Road was also more reliable since it was less affected by changes in the weather and was built for speedy travel by horse. For the Achaemenid Empire, the Royal Road was a way to deliver messages quickly, supplement trade, and ensure the king had eyes all over his vast empire.

The Royal Road was not the only highway through which commerce was possible. The Great Khurasan Road connected Mesopotamia to the Iranian Plateau and then ran as far as the Indus Valley. It functioned as an unofficial alternate route for merchants and later became a route for cultural exchange after the conquest of Alexander the Great. During the Abbasid dynasty, the Khurasan Road became part of the Silk Road.

Conclusion

The Achaemenid Empire holds great significance even today, not only as the largest empire of its time to exist but also due to the lasting influence it had on the geopolitical makeup of the Iranian Plateau. Beginning with Cyrus the Great, the Persian Empire came to hold great importance. As the empire expanded, it gathered power and wealth.

With the diverse regions the Achaemenids were able to conquer, the Persian Empire assimilated many different cultures, religions, and languages. It also introduced the Persians to more efficient forms of governance, superior military techniques and weaponry, and laborers skilled in many crafts. The Achaemenid Empire's power can be seen by the monuments they left behind, which were inscribed with tales of their successes. In the empire's early years, it saw much success and remained a hallmark of diversity and tolerance.

Even after the empire fell to the Greeks, it continued to have a lasting effect on the region. Persian heritage and culture went on to hold great relevance in Asia and the Middle East, where it was assimilated by other empires and dynasties. Many of the Persian Empire's policies can be seen in later empires.

Alexander the Great's conquest of the Persian Empire brought him a vast land, which he was free to rule as he saw fit, yet the Greeks chose to continue with the Persian form of governance. Later, the Romans would adopt a similar method. The Persian governance model was adopted by the Abbasid dynasty in the mid-8th century CE during a period known as the Golden Age of Islam. The Abbasids followed the Achaemenid custom of setting up an empire center in Mesopotamia and were largely supported by the Persian aristocracy during their rise and expansion. The Persian language and architecture went to become heavily incorporated into the Islamic world.

While the Achaemenid Empire preached and practiced religious tolerance, it is difficult to determine the motive behind such a move. It may simply have been for the sake of acceptance and diversity, or it may be that it would have been practically impossible to enforce any single religion, culture, or language over such a vast empire; any attempt to do so likely would have disrupted the peace. Regardless, this approach set an example of religious tolerance and acceptance that is still hailed as a mark of a great ruler today. The impact of the religious policies of the Achaemenid emperors, in particular, their support of the Jews who were conquered and forced away from their homes by the Babylonians, earned them a mention in Judeo-Christian texts.

Since the Achaemenid emperors are believed to have practiced Zoroastrianism, or at least some of its teachings, they played a vital role in its spread. The empire was home to a large number of Zoroastrian followers, and with the expansion of the empire, the Persians were introduced to new cultures and religions. However, they also brought Zoroastrianism to the regions they conquered, along with neighboring territories. Due to the Persians, Zoroastrianism spread as far as China, where it thrived for close to a millennium until the Tang dynasty persecuted its practitioners.

The Persians are seen as the major instigators of the Greco-Persian Wars, and they greatly influenced the culture of Greek regions. The Athenians, for example, adopted many Persian customs and traditions into their daily lives. While the nature of the relationship between the two groups was often hostile, it did not prevent the two from engaging in a sort of cultural exchange, resulting in the development of new hybrid customs.

The Persian Empire's initial success seems just as inevitable as its later doom. The empire had begun with a clear vision and purpose, which Cyrus the Great and his successors put into action. The expansion of the empire was not simply a matter of waging wars; the emperors were also concerned with just and equal governance, tolerance, and kindness. Later rulers of the empire may be entirely responsible for the empire's fall, as the focus shifted from the empire's prosperity to fights for the throne, resulting in brothers waging wars and killing each other. Although the Achaemenid Empire attempted to reestablish its dominance, it did so by picking fights it was ill-equipped to win, resulting in its disastrous but inescapable demise. However, its legacy will live on.

Here's another book by Enthralling History
that you might like

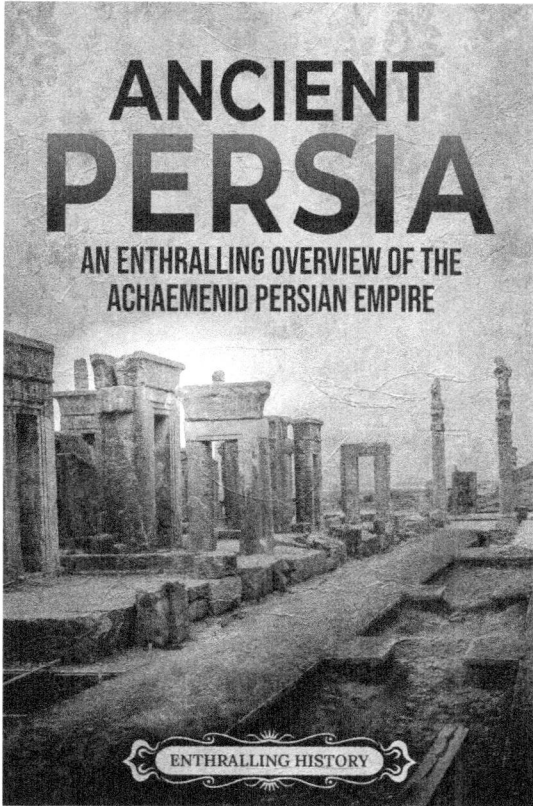

Free limited time bonus

Stop for a moment. We have a free bonus set up for you. The problem is this: we forget 90% of everything that we read after 7 days. Crazy fact, right? Here's the solution: we've created a printable, 1-page pdf summary for this book that you're reading now. All you have to do to get your free pdf summary is to go to the following website:

https://livetolearn.lpages.co/enthrallinghistory/

Once you do, it will be intuitive. Enjoy, and thank you!

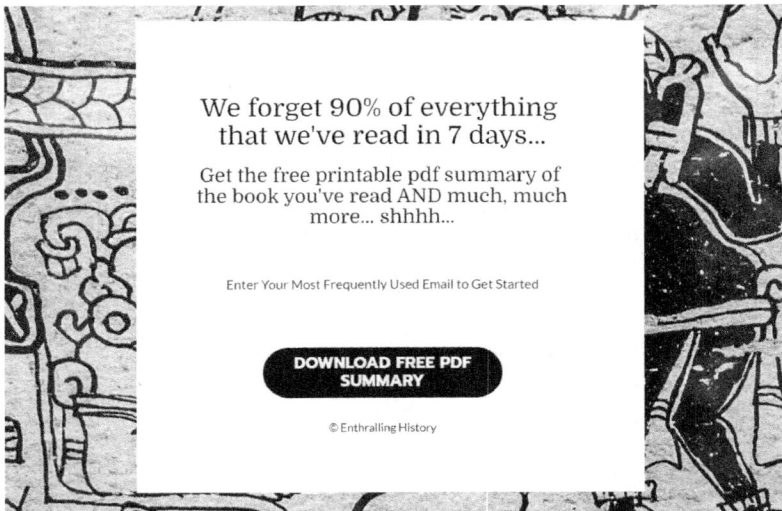

We forget 90% of everything that we've read in 7 days...

Get the free printable pdf summary of the book you've read AND much, much more... shhhh...

Enter Your Most Frequently Used Email to Get Started

DOWNLOAD FREE PDF SUMMARY

© Enthralling History

Bibliography

Al Atrash, Sami. "The Rise and Fall of the Scythians in Western Asia." TheCollector, 14 July 2022, https://www.thecollector.com/rise-of-the-scythians/.

Arteshe Iran. "Siege of Pasargadae Hill." Arteshe Iran - Persian Military History, 2009, http://arteshe-iran.blogspot.com/2009/01/siege-of-pasargadae-hill.html

Badian, E. "Darius III." Harvard Studies in Classical Philology, vol. 1000, 2000, pp. 241–267. JSTOR, https://doi.org/10.2307/3185218.

Baldwin, Tanya. "Cyrus the Great Facts & Achievements | Who was King Cyrus the Great? - Video & Lesson Transcript." Study.com, 26 April 2022, https://study.com/learn/lesson/cyrus-the-great-facts-achievements.html.

Bawden, Charles R. "Darius III | king of Persia | Britannica." Encyclopedia Britannica, 1 January 2023, https://www.britannica.com/biography/Darius-III.

Behroozi, Mehrnaaz, and Leila Kochaki Kia. "The Administrative Structure of Achaemenid and Seleucid Empires in Observing Civil Rights." International Journal of Culture and History, vol. 3, no. 1, 2017, http://www.ijch.net/vol3/077-SD0018.pdf.

BlueBox Creighton. "Art and Architecture of the Achaemenid Empire." BlueBox Creighton, 2016, https://bluebox.creighton.edu/demo/modules/en-boundless-old/www.boundless.com/art-history/textbooks/boundless-art-history-textbook/art-of-the-ancient-near-east-3/persia-863/art-and-architecture-of-the-achaemenid-empire-292-1911/.

Bosanquet, I. W. "Chronology of the Medes, from the Reign of Deioces to the Reign of Darius, the Son of Hystaspes, or Darius the Mede." Journal of the Royal Asiatic Society of Great Britain and Ireland, vol. 17, 1860, pp. 39-69. JSTOR, https://www.jstor.org/stable/25581223?seq=6.

Bowman, Alan K., et al. "Ancient Egypt | History, Government, Culture, Map, & Facts." Encyclopedia Britannica, 3 January 2023, https://www.britannica.com/place/ancient-Egypt.

Briant, Pierre. "Darius II." Oxford Classical Dictionary, 10 August 2022, https://oxfordre.com/classics/display/10.1093/acrefore/9780199381135.001.0001/acrefore-9780199381135-e-2030;jsessionid=B1D1E132F1430380405FB5B68CE2294D.

Briant, Pierre. From Cyrus to Alexander: A History of the Persian Empire. Pennsylvania State University Press, 2002.

Britannica, The Editors of Encyclopedia. "Ancient Iran | History, Map, Cities, Religion, Art, Language, & Facts." Encyclopedia Britannica, 2022, https://www.britannica.com/place/ancient-Iran.

Britannica, The Editors of Encyclopedia. "Battle of Issus." Encyclopedia Britannica, 4 January 2023, https://www.britannica.com/event/Battle-of-Issus-Persian-history

Britannica, The Editors of Encyclopedia. "Deioces | king of Media | Britannica." Encyclopedia Britannica, 2016, https://www.britannica.com/biography/Deioces.

Britannica, The Editors of Encyclopedia. "Greco-Persian Wars | Definition, Battles, Summary, Facts, Effects, & History." Encyclopedia Britannica, 2022, https://www.britannica.com/event/Greco-Persian-Wars.

Britannica, The Editors of Encyclopedia. "Greco-Persian Wars | Definition, Battles, Summary, Facts, Effects, & History." Encyclopedia Britannica, 2022, https://www.britannica.com/event/Greco-Persian-Wars.

Britannica, The Editors of Encyclopedia. "Magus | Persian priesthood | Britannica." Encyclopedia Britannica, 2022, https://www.britannica.com/topic/Magus.

Britannica, The Editors of Encyclopedia. "Media | ancient region, Iran | Britannica." Encyclopedia Britannica, 2020, https://www.britannica.com/place/Media-ancient-region-Iran.

Britannica, The Editors of Encyclopedia. "Battle of Cnidus | Persian history | Britannica." Encyclopedia Britannica, 2022, https://www.britannica.com/topic/Battle-of-Cnidus.

Cartwright, Mark. "Lydia." World History Encyclopedia, 3 April 2016, https://www.worldhistory.org/lydia/.

Charles, Michael. "TWO NOTES ON DARIUS III." The Cambridge Classical Journal, vol. 62, 2016, pp. 52-64, https://doi.org/10.1017/S1750270516000063.

Chua, Michelle. "The Strength and Structure of the Ancient Persian Army." Brewminate, 21 June 2019, https://brewminate.com/the-strength-and-structure-of-the-ancient-persian-army/.

The Columbia Encyclopedia. "Artaxerxes II." Encyclopedia.com, 2023, https://www.encyclopedia.com/reference/encyclopedias-almanacs-transcripts-and-maps/artaxerxes-ii.

The Columbia Encyclopedia. "Darius II." Encyclopedia.com, The Columbia Encyclopedia, 2023, https://www.encyclopedia.com/reference/encyclopedias-almanacs-transcripts-and-maps/darius-ii.

Course Hero. "Histories Book 5 The Persian Conquest of Thrace Summary." Course Hero, 2019, https://www.coursehero.com/lit/Histories/book-5-the-persian-conquest-of-thrace-summary/.

Criss, Megan. "Achaemenid Art & Architecture: Definition & Characteristics." Study.com, 2016, https://study.com/academy/lesson/achaemenid-art-architecture-definition-characteristics.html.

Cristian, Radu, and Osama Shukir. "Darius I." World History Encyclopedia, 10 April 2017, https://www.worldhistory.org/Darius_I/.

Crystalinks. "Median Empire." Crystalinks, 2023, https://www.crystalinks.com/media.html.

Cyrus, Emperor, and Reza Abbasi. "Persian Art - A History of Ancient Persian Paintings and Iranian Art." Art in Context, 28 June 2022, https://artincontext.org/persian-art/.

Dandamayev, M. A. "ARTABAZUS – Encyclopedia Iranica." Encyclopedia Iranica, 1986, https://iranicaonline.org/articles/artabazus-gk.

Dandamayev, Muhammad A. "CAMBYSES – Encyclopedia Iranica." Encyclopedia Iranica, 1990, https://www.iranicaonline.org/articles/cambyses-opers.

Dandamayev, Muhammad A. "MAGI – Encyclopedia Iranica." Encyclopedia Iranica, 30 May 2000, https://www.iranicaonline.org/articles/magi.

Deering, Mary. "Persian Empire Timeline & Culture | When Did the Persian Empire Start? - Video & Lesson Transcript." Study.com, 20 January 2022, https://study.com/academy/lesson/persian-empire-history-culture-timeline.html.

Department of Ancient Near Eastern Art. "Assyria, 1365–609 B.C. | Essay." The Metropolitan Museum of Art, 2004, https://www.metmuseum.org/toah/hd/assy/hd_assy.htm.

Ducksters. "Iran History and Timeline Overview." Ducksters, Technological Solutions, 2023, https://www.ducksters.com/geography/country/iran_history_timeline.php.

Dunn, Jimmy. "Egypt: Cambyses II, the First Persian Ruler of Egypt and His Lost Army." Tour Egypt, 12 June 2011, http://www.touregypt.net/featurestories/cambyses2.htm.

Encyclopedia Iranica. "ARTAXERXES I – Encyclopedia Iranica." Encyclopedia Iranica, 2011, https://www.iranicaonline.org/articles/artaxerxes-i.

Encyclopedia Judaica. "Medes and Media." Jewish Virtual Library, 2008, https://www.jewishvirtuallibrary.org/medes-and-media.

Encyclopedia of Ancient Art. "Ancient Persian Art & Culture." Visual Arts Cork, 2022, http://www.visual-arts-cork.com/ancient-art/persian.htm.

The Famous People. "Artaxerxes I Of Persia Biography - Facts, Childhood, Family Life & Achievements." The Famous People, 2020, https://www.thefamouspeople.com/profiles/artaxerxes-i-of-persia-37603.php.

"From Artaxerxes III to Alexander III, 342–332." Trouble in the West: Egypt and the Persian Empire, 525-332 BC, by Stephen Ruzicka, Oxford University Press, USA, 2012, pp. 199-209.

Frye, Richard N., and Matthew Smith. "Cyrus the Great | Biography & Facts | Britannica." Encyclopedia Britannica, 6 January 2023, https://www.britannica.com/biography/Cyrus-the-Great

Garlinghouse, Tom. "Who were the ancient Persians?" Live Science, 14 July 2022, https://www.livescience.com/who-were-the-persians.

Gill, NS. "Ancient Persian Rulers Timeline (Modern Iran)." ThoughtCo, 30 May 2019, https://www.thoughtco.com/timeline-of-the-ancient-rulers-of-persia-120250.

Gill, NS. "The Battle at Issus." ThoughtCo, 6 September 2018, https://www.thoughtco.com/overview-battle-issus-november-333-bc-116810.

Giotto, M. "The Peloponnesian Wars ("The Great War" 431-404 BC)." Penfield Edu, 2013, https://www.penfield.edu/webpages/jgiotto/onlinetextbook.cfm?subpage=164984 9.

GotQuestions. "Who was Artaxerxes in the Bible?" GotQuestions.org, 25 February 2022, https://www.gotquestions.org/Artaxerxes-in-the-Bible.html.

Gottheil, Richard, and Eduard Meyer. "ARTAXERXES III. - JewishEncyclopedia.com." Jewish Encyclopedia, 2023, https://www.jewishencyclopedia.com/articles/1829-artaxerxes-iii.

Gottheil, Richard, and Eduard Meyer. "ARTAXERXES II - JewishEncyclopedia.com." Jewish Encyclopedia, 2022, https://www.jewishencyclopedia.com/articles/1828-artaxerxes-ii.

Gottheil, Richard, and Eduard Meyer. "ARTAXERXES I - JewishEncyclopedia.com." Jewish Encyclopedia, 2023, https://www.jewishencyclopedia.com/articles/1827-artaxerxes-i.

Harding, Robert. "The Battle of Gaugamela, 1 October 331 BC." The Past, 8 September 2021, https://the-past.com/feature/the-battle-of-gaugamela-1-october-331-bc/.

Heritage History. "Persian Wars of Conquest." Heritage History, 2022, https://www.heritage-history.com/index.php?c=resources&s=war-dir&f=wars_persianconquest.

Hirschy, Noah Calvin. Artaxerxes III Ochus and His Reign: With Special Consideration of the Old Testament Sources Bearing Upon the Period; An Inaugural Dissertation (Classic Reprint). Fb&c Limited, 2016.

History.com Editors. "Peloponnesian War." History, 22 August 2019, https://www.history.com/topics/ancient-greece/peloponnesian-war.

HIstory.com Editors. "Zoroastrianism." History.com, 13 February 2018, https://www.history.com/topics/religion/zoroastrianism. Accessed 19 February 2023.

History World. "History of Iran (Persia)." HistoryWorld, 2023, http://www.historyworld.net/wrldhis/PlainTextHistories.asp?ParagraphID=azt.

Hodsdon, Edd. "Darius the Great: 9 Facts About the King of Kings." TheCollector, 5 February 2021, https://www.thecollector.com/darius-the-great-king-of-kings/.

Hodsdon, Edd. "King Xerxes I: 9 Facts About His Life and Rule." TheCollector, 26 February 2021, https://www.thecollector.com/king-xerxes-i/.

Holmes, Robert CL. "Kings of Persia: These 12 Achaemenid Rulers Led an Empire." TheCollector, 18 July 2020, https://www.thecollector.com/kings-of-persia/.

Homepages. "Artaxerxes II King of Persia." Homepages, 2003, https://homepages.rpi.edu/~holmes/Hobbies/Genealogy2/ps22/ps22_441.htm.

Homepages. "Xerxes I 'The Great' King of Persia." Homepages, 2003, https://homepages.rpi.edu/~holmes/Hobbies/Genealogy2/ps22/ps22_444.htm.

Horne, Charles F. "Ancient Mesopotamia: Biography of Cyrus the Great." Ducksters, 2023, https://www.ducksters.com/history/mesopotamia/cyrus_the_great.php.

Hyland, John O., and Stephen Ruzicka. "Persian Interventions | Hopkins Press." JHU Press, 2017, https://www.press.jhu.edu/books/title/11954/persian-interventions.

Iran Chamber Society. "Historic Personalities of Iran: Median Empire." Iran Chamber Society, 2023, https://www.iranchamber.com/history/median/median.php.

Iran Chamber Society. "History of Iran: Cyrus the Great." Iran Chamber Society, 2023, https://www.iranchamber.com/history/cyrus/cyrus.php.

Iran Chamber Society. "History of Iran: Darius the Great." Iran Chamber Society, 2023, https://www.iranchamber.com/history/darius/darius.php.

Jameson, Zachary, and Stephanie Przybylek. "Persian Empire Architecture & Art | What was the Persian Empire? - Video & Lesson Transcript." Study.com, 28 July 2022, https://study.com/learn/lesson/persian-empire-architecture-art.html.

Joe, Jimmy. "Darius III: The Last King of the Great Persian Empire." Timeless Myths, 2022, https://www.timelessmyths.com/characters/darius-iii/.

Joe, Jimmy. "Darius II: The Authentic Legacy of This Persian King of Kings." Timeless Myths, 2022, https://www.timelessmyths.com/characters/darius-ii/.

Kennedy, Stetson. "Cyrus the Great and Religious Tolerance | Tolerance." Tolerance: Tavaana, 2022, https://tolerance.tavaana.org/en/content/cyrus-great-and-religious-tolerance.

Kerrigan, Michael. "Battle of Nineveh | Summary | Britannica." Encyclopedia Britannica, 2017, https://www.britannica.com/event/Battle-of-Nineveh.

Khan Academy. "The Rise of Persia (article)." Khan Academy, 2017, https://www.khanacademy.org/humanities/world-history/ancient-medieval/ancient-persia/a/the-rise-of-persia.

Kidd, Fiona. "Ideas of Empire: The "Royal Garden" at Pasargadae." Metropolitan Museum of Art, 29 July 2013, https://www.metmuseum.org/blogs/now-at-the-met/features/2013/pasargadae.

Klein, Christopher. "How Cyrus the Great Turned Ancient Persia into a Superpower." How Cyrus the Great Turned Ancient Persia into a Superpower, 14 July 2022, https://www.history.com/news/cyrus-the-great-persian-empire-iran.

Klein, Christopher. "How Cyrus the Great Turned Ancient Persia into a Superpower." How Cyrus the Great Turned Ancient Persia into a Superpower, 14 July 2022, https://www.history.com/news/cyrus-the-great-persian-empire-iran.

Kohansal, Hassan. "The Function of Non- Iranian Languages in the Persian Achaemenid Empire | PalArch's Journal of Archaeology of Egypt / Egyptology." PalArch's Journals, 30 December 2020, https://archives.palarch.nl/index.php/jae/article/view/8871.

Kovalev, R. K. "Scythians." Encyclopedia.com, 2018, https://www.encyclopedia.com/history/modern-europe/russian-soviet-and-cis-history/scythians.

Landious Travel. "Artaxerxes III." Landious Travel, 2023, https://landioustravel.com/egypt/pharaohs-egypt/artaxerxes-iii/.

The Latin Library. "The Persian Empire." The Latin Library, 2023, http://www.thelatinlibrary.com/imperialism/notes/persia.html.

Lendering, Jona. "Amyrtaeus." Livius.org, 30 April 2020, https://www.livius.org/articles/person/amyrtaeus/.

Lendering, Jona. "Artabazus (2)." Livius.org, 4 August 2020, https://www.livius.org/articles/person/artabazus-2/.

Lendering, Jona. "Cambyses II." Livius.org, 30 April 2020, https://www.livius.org/articles/person/cambyses-ii/.

Lendering, Jona. "Cambyses II." Livius.org, 30 April 2020, https://www.livius.org/articles/person/cambyses-ii/.

Lendering, Jona. "Cambyses II (2)." Livius.org, 23 June 2020, https://www.livius.org/articles/person/cambyses-ii/cambyses-ii-2/.

Lendering, Jona. "Cyaxares." Livius.org, 9 May 2019, https://www.livius.org/articles/person/cyaxares/.

Lendering, Jona. "Cyrus the Great." Livius.org, 12 October 2020, https://www.livius.org/articles/person/cyrus-the-great/.

Lendering, Jona. "Darius II Nothus." Livius.org, 12 October 2020, https://www.livius.org/articles/person/darius-ii-nothus/.

Lendering, Jona. "Darius the Great: Death." Livius.org, 21 April 2020, https://www.livius.org/articles/person/darius-the-great/9-death/.

Lendering, Jona. "Medes." Livius.org, 12 October 2020, https://www.livius.org/articles/people/medes/.

Lendering, Jona. "Mycale (479 BCE)." Livius.org, 10 August 2020, https://www.livius.org/articles/battle/mycale-479-bce/.

Lendering, Jona. "Persepolis, Hall of 100 Columns." Livius.org, 23 April 2020, https://www.livius.org/articles/place/persepolis/persepolis-photos/persepolis-hall-of-100-columns/.

Library of Congress. "Religion - A Thousand Years of the Persian Book | Exhibitions." Library of Congress, 2022, https://www.loc.gov/exhibits/thousand-years-of-the-persian-book/religion.html.

Livius. "The treaties between Persia and Sparta." Livius.org, 15 October 2020, https://www.livius.org/sources/content/thucydides-historian/the-treaties-between-persia-and-sparta/.

Lloyd, H. F. "Iranian art and architecture | ancient art | Britannica." Encyclopedia Britannica, 2018, https://www.britannica.com/art/Iranian-art.

Lohnes, Kate, and Donald Sommerville. "Battle of Thermopylae | Date, Location, and Facts." Encyclopedia Britannica, 12 February 2023, https://www.britannica.com/event/Battle-of-Thermopylae-Greek-history-480-BC.

Lorenzi, Rossella. "Vanished Persian army said found in desert." NBC News, 9 November 2009, https://www.nbcnews.com/id/wbna33791672.

Lumen Learning. "Government and Trade in the Achaemenid Empire | World Civilization." Lumen Learning, 2022, https://courses.lumenlearning.com/suny-hccc-worldcivilization/chapter/government-and-trade-in-the-achaemenid-empire/.

Mark, Joshua J. "The Battle of Pelusium: A Victory Decided by Cats." World History Encyclopedia, 13 June 2017, https://www.worldhistory.org/article/43/the-battle-of-pelusium-a-victory-decided-by-cats/.

Mark, Joshua J., et al. "Ancient Persian Art and Architecture." World History Encyclopedia, 22 January 2020, https://www.worldhistory.org/Ancient_Persian_Art_and_Architecture/.

Mark, Joshua J., et al. "Ancient Persian Government." World History Encyclopedia, 14 November 2019, https://www.worldhistory.org/Persian_Government/.

Mark, Joshua J., et al. "Ancient Persian Warfare." World History Encyclopedia, 25 November 2019, https://www.worldhistory.org/Persian_Warfare/.

Mark, Joshua J., et al. "Artaxerxes II." World History Encyclopedia, 6 March 2020, https://www.worldhistory.org/Artaxerxes_II/.

Mark, Joshua J., et al. "Battle of Thymbra." World History Encyclopedia, 3 November 2022, https://www.worldhistory.org/Battle_of_Thymbra/.

Mark, Joshua J., et al. "Xerxes I." World History Encyclopedia, 2018, https://www.worldhistory.org/Xerxes_I/.

Mark, Joshua J., and Bruce Allardice. "Artaxerxes II." World History Encyclopedia, 6 March 2020, https://www.worldhistory.org/Artaxerxes_II/.

Mark, Joshua J., and Mark Cartwright. "Artaxerxes I." World History Encyclopedia, 3 March 2020, https://www.worldhistory.org/Artaxerxes_I/.

Mark, Joshua J., and Marc De Mieroop. "Behistun Inscription." World History Encyclopedia, 28 November 2019, https://www.worldhistory.org/Behistun_Inscription/.

Mark, Joshua J., and Katarina Maruskinova. "Elam." World History Encyclopedia, 27 August 2020, https://www.worldhistory.org/elam/.

Mark, Joshua J., and Osama Shukir. "Ancient Persian Religion." World History Encyclopedia, 11 December 2019, https://www.worldhistory.org/Ancient_Persian_Religion/.

Mark, Joshua J., and Osama Shukir. "Assyria." World History Encyclopedia, 2018, https://www.worldhistory.org/assyria/.

Matthews, Rupert. "Battle of Gaugamela." Encyclopedia Britannica, 4 January 2023, https://www.britannica.com/event/Battle-of-Gaugamela.

Matthews, Rupert. "Battle of Granicus | Summary | Britannica." Encyclopedia Britannica, 2017, https://www.britannica.com/event/Battle-of-the-Granicus-334BCE.

Maurino, M. "Battle of Opis - The Great Battles of History." Ars Bellica, 2014, http://www.arsbellica.it/pagine/battaglie_in_sintesi/Opis_eng.html. Accessed 16 February 2023.

McCollum, Daniel. "The Persian Empire: Government & Army - Video & Lesson Transcript." Study.com, 28 December 2021, https://study.com/academy/lesson/the-persian-empire-government-army.html.

McGill. "Cyrus the Great." Cyrus the Great, 2023, https://www.cs.mcgill.ca/~rwest/wikispeedia/wpcd/wp/c/Cyrus_the_Great.htm.

The Met Museum. "Relief: figure in a procession." MetMuseum, 2017.

Mildenberg, Leo. "Artaxerxes III Ochus (358 – 338 B.C.). A Note on the Maligned King." Zeitschrift Des Deutschen Palästina-Vereins, vol. 115, no. 2, 1999, pp. 201-227. JSTOR, http://www.jstor.org/stable/27931620.

Military History. "Artaxerxes III." Military Wiki, 2022, https://military-history.fandom.com/wiki/Artaxerxes_III.

Military History. "Battle of Pasargadae | Military Wiki | Fandom." Military Wiki, 2023, https://military-history.fandom.com/wiki/Battle_of_Pasargadae.

Ministry. "Research: The Seventh Year of Artaxerxes I." Ministry Magazine, 1953, https://www.ministrymagazine.org/archive/1953/06/research-the-seventh-year-of-artaxerxes-i.

Munn, JM. "Darius I | Biography, Accomplishments, & Facts | Britannica." Encyclopedia Britannica, 2022, https://www.britannica.com/biography/Darius-I.

Muscarella, O. W. "IRON AGE." Encyclopedia Iranica, 15 December 2006, https://www.iranicaonline.org/articles/iron-age.

Muscato, Christopher. "Persian Empire: Religion & Social Structure | History & Significance - Video & Lesson Transcript." Study.com, 19 April 2022, https://study.com/academy/lesson/the-persian-empire-religion-social-structure.html.

National Geographic Society. "The Peloponnesian War." National Geographic Society, 19 May 2022, https://education.nationalgeographic.org/resource/peloponnesian-war.

New World Encyclopedia. "Cyrus the Great." New World Encyclopedia, 23 June 2022, https://www.newworldencyclopedia.org/entry/Cyrus_the_Great.

Nijssen, Daan, and Larry Hedrick. "Cyrus the Great." World History Encyclopedia, 21 February 2018, https://www.worldhistory.org/Cyrus_the_Great/.

Nijssen, Daan, and Simon Seitz. "Cambyses II." World History Encyclopedia, 18 May 2018, https://www.worldhistory.org/Cambyses_II/.

Nikiforov, Leonid Alekseyevich. "Phraortes | king of Media | Britannica." Encyclopedia Britannica, 4 February 2023, https://www.britannica.com/biography/Phraortes.

"Pasargadae | For UNESCO World Heritage Travellers." World Heritage Site, 2022, https://www.worldheritagesite.org/list/Pasargadae.

Peel, Mike. "Cyrus the Great Biography - The Great King of Persia." Totally History, 2013, https://totallyhistory.com/cyrus-the-great/.

Penner, Jay. "The Story of the Lost Army of Cambyses." Jay Penner Books, 2020, https://jaypenner.com/blog/the-story-of-the-lost-army-of-cambyses/.

The Persians. "Iran, the world's first superpower." The Persians, 2018, https://www.the-persians.co.uk/medes.htm.

The Persians. "IRAN: The world's first superpower." The Persians, 10 August 2022, https://www.the-persians.co.uk/.well-known/captcha/?r=%2FartaxerxesII.1.htm.

The Persians. "IRAN The world's first superpower." The Persians, 10 August 2022, https://www.the-persians.co.uk/.well-known/captcha/?r=%2FartaxerxesII.1.htm.

Persians Are Not Arabs. "Persian Architecture • Evolution of modern art (& famous buildings) | PANA." Persians Are Not Arabs, 2019, https://www.persiansarenotarabs.com/persian-architecture/.

PressBooks. "Persian Art – Art and Visual Culture: Prehistory to Renaissance." PressBooks, 2023, https://pressbooks.bccampus.ca/cavestocathedrals/chapter/persian/.

Przybylek, Stephanie. "The Persian Empire: Art & Architecture - Video & Lesson Transcript." Study.com, 31 December 2022, https://study.com/academy/lesson/the-persian-empire-art-architecture.html.

Public Broadcasting Service. "The Greeks - Sparta and Persia strike up an alliance in 413." PBS, 2023, http://www.pbs.org/empires/thegreeks/keyevents/412_c.html.

Radpour, Ardeshir, and Andre Castaigne. "Achaemenid Military Equipments | CAIS©." The Circle of Ancient Iranian Studies, 2022, https://www.cais-soas.com/CAIS/History/hakhamaneshian/AchaemenidMilitaryEquip.htm.

Rahnamoon, Fariborz. "History of Persian or Parsi Language." Iran Chamber Society, 2023, https://www.iranchamber.com/literature/articles/persian_parsi_language_history.php.

Rattini, Kristin Baird. "Darius I—facts and information." National Geographic, 11 February 2019, https://www.nationalgeographic.com/culture/article/darius-i-persia.

Rattini, Kristin Baird. "Who was Cyrus the Great?" National Geographic, 6 May 2019, https://www.nationalgeographic.com/culture/article/cyrus-the-great.

"The Religion of Xerxes." Xerxes: A Persian Life, by Richard Stoneman, Yale University Press, 2015, pp. 88-108.

Rensselaer Polytechnic Institute. "Cyaxares King of the Medes." Rensselaer Polytechnic Institute, https://homepages.rpi.edu/~holmes/Hobbies/Genealogy2/ps22/ps22_460.htm.

Rezakhani, Khodad. "Medes, the First (Western) Iranian Kingdom - (The Circle of Ancient Iranian Studies - CAIS)©." CAIS @ SOAS, 2023, https://www.cais-soas.com/CAIS/History/madha/medes_first_iranian_kingdom.htm.

Rickard, J. "Artaxerxes III, r.359-338 BC." History of War, 14 September 2016, http://www.historyofwar.org/articles/people_artaxerxes_III.html.

Rickard, J. "Artaxerxes II (r.404-359 BC)." History of War, 14 September 2016, http://www.historyofwar.org/articles/people_artaxerxes_II.html.

Rickard, J. "Darius II, r.423-404 BC." History of War, 6 April 2017, http://www.historyofwar.org/articles/people_darius_II.html.

Rickard, J. "Persian Conquest of Egypt, 525 BC." History of War, 24 March 2015, http://www.historyofwar.org/articles/wars_persian_egypt_525.html.

Ronan, Mark. "The Rise and Fall of Nimrud." History Today, 6 June 2015, https://www.historytoday.com/archive/history-matters/rise-and-fall-nimrud.

Ryder, T. T.B. "Spartan Relations with Persia after the King's Peace: A Strange Story in Diodorus 15.9." The Classical Quarterly, vol. 13, no. 1, 1963, pp. 105-109. JSTOR, https://www.jstor.org/stable/637943.

Sancisi-Weerdenburg, Heleen. "DARIUS iv. Darius II – Encyclopedia Iranica." Encyclopedia Iranica, 1994, https://iranicaonline.org/articles/darius-iv.

Savoia, Gianpaolo. "The Median Dynastic Empire; The Coming of the Aryans & Creation of the First Iranian Dynastic Empire | CAIS©." CAIS @ SOAS, 2004, https://www.cais-soas.com/CAIS/History/madha/medes.htm.

Schmitt, R. "ARTAXERXES II – Encyclopedia Iranica." Encyclopedia Iranica, 1986, https://www.iranicaonline.org/articles/artaxerxes-ii-achaemenid-king.

Schmitt, R. "ARTAXERXES III – Encyclopedia Iranica." Encyclopedia Iranica, 1986, https://www.iranicaonline.org/articles/artaxerxes-iii-throne-name-of-ochus-gk.

Schmitt, R. "ASTYAGES – Encyclopedia Iranica." Encyclopedia Iranica, 1987, https://iranicaonline.org/articles/astyages-the-last-median-king.

Schmitt, Rüdiger. "DEIOCES." Encyclopedia Iranica, 17 January 2022, https://www.iranicaonline.org/articles/deioces.

Scmitt, R. "ASTYAGES – Encyclopedia Iranica." Encyclopedia Iranica, 2011, https://iranicaonline.org/articles/astyages-the-last-median-king.

Seymour, Michael. "The Later Legacy of Cyrus the Great." The Metropolitan Museum of Art, 24 June 2013, https://www.metmuseum.org/blogs/now-at-the-met/features/2013/cyrus-the-great.

Shahbazi, A. S. "History of Iran: Achaemenid Army." Iran Chamber Society, 2023, https://www.iranchamber.com/history/achaemenids/achaemenid_army.php.

Shannahan, John. "Artaxerxes II." Macquarie University, 28 March 2022, https://figshare.mq.edu.au/articles/thesis/Artaxerxes_II/19443077/1.

Shapur Shahbazi, A. "DARIUS iii. Darius I the Great – Encyclopedia Iranica." Encyclopedia Iranica, 1994, https://iranicaonline.org/articles/darius-iii.

Smith, Matthew. "Artaxerxes I | king of Persia | Britannica." Encyclopedia Britannica, 20 January 2023, https://www.britannica.com/biography/Artaxerxes-I.

Smith, Matthew. "Astyages | king of Media | Britannica." Encyclopedia Britannica, 20 January 2023, https://www.britannica.com/biography/Astyages.

Smith, Matthew. "Cambyses II | king of Persia | Britannica." Encyclopedia Britannica, 20 January 2023, https://www.britannica.com/biography/Cambyses-II.

Smith, Matthew. "Croesus | king of Lydia | Britannica." Encyclopedia Britannica, 20 January 2023, https://www.britannica.com/biography/Croesus.

Smith, Matthew. "Cyaxares | king of Media | Britannica." Encyclopedia Britannica, 20 January 2023, https://www.britannica.com/biography/Cyaxares.

Smith, Matthew. "Darius II Ochus | king of Persia | Britannica." Encyclopedia Britannica, 20 January 2023, https://www.britannica.com/biography/Darius-II-Ochus.

Smith, Scott, and Adrienne Mayor. "Scythian Warfare." World History Encyclopedia, 21 February 2022, https://www.worldhistory.org/Scythian_Warfare/.

Sommerville, Donald. "Battle of Plataea | Summary | Britannica." Encyclopedia Britannica, 2017, https://www.britannica.com/event/Battle-of-Plataea.

Stewart, M. "People, Places, & Things: Medes." Greek Mythology: From the Iliad to the Fall of the Last Tyrant, 2023, http://messagenetcommresearch.com/myths/ppt/Medes_1.html.

Sullivan, Richard E. "Artaxerxes III | king of Persia | Britannica." Encyclopedia Britannica, 31 January 2023, https://www.britannica.com/biography/Artaxerxes-III.

Sullivan, Richard E. "Artaxerxes II | king of Persia | Britannica." Encyclopedia Britannica, 31 January 2023, https://www.britannica.com/biography/Artaxerxes-II.

TAPPersia. "A History of Persian Art and Architecture." TAP Persia, 12 November 2022, https://www.tappersia.com/a-history-of-persian-art-and-architecture/.

"10. The Mythical Origins of the Medes and the Persians." Myth, Truth, and Narrative in Herodotus, edited by Emily Baragwanath and Mathieu de Bakker, OUP Oxford, 2012.

ThenAgain. "Darius III: 336-330 BC." thenagain.info, 2022, http://www.thenagain.info/WebChron/MiddleEast/DariusIII.html.

Time Graphics. "Artaxerxes I (Longimanus) King of Persia 475 - 423 B.C.E. (Nov 3, 475 BC – Feb 19, 423 BC) (Timeline)." Time Graphics, 2018, https://time.graphics/period/219447.

TimeMaps. "The Persian Empire: Government and State in Ancient Persia." TimeMaps, 2022, https://timemaps.com/encyclopedia/persian-empire-state/.

Truitt, Benjamin. "King Cyrus the Great: Biography & Accomplishments - Video & Lesson Transcript." Study.com, 14 September 2021, https://study.com/academy/lesson/cyrus-the-great-facts-accomplishments-quiz.html.

Twinkl. "What is Persian Religion? - Answered." Twinkl, 2022, https://www.twinkl.com.pk/teaching-wiki/persian-religion.

UC Santa Barbara. "History of Persian Language." Persian Languages and Literature at UCSB, 2017, https://persian.religion.ucsb.edu/home/history-of-persian/.

U*X*L Encyclopedia of World Mythology. "Persian Mythology." Encyclopedia.com, 2023, https://www.encyclopedia.com/history/encyclopedias-almanacs-transcripts-and-maps/persian-mythology.

Walvoord, John F. "6. The Medes and The Persians." Bible.org, 1 January 2008, https://bible.org/seriespage/6-medes-and-persians.

Wasson, Donald L., and Ruth Sheppard. "Battle of the Granicus." World History Encyclopedia, 20 December 2011, https://www.worldhistory.org/Battle_of_the_Granicus/.

Waterfield, Robin. "Darius the Great Conquers the Indus Valley." WikiSummaries, 11 November 2022, https://wikisummaries.org/darius-the-great-conquers-the-indus-valley/.

Waters, Matt, and Simeon Netchev. "Cyrus the Great's Conquests." World History Encyclopedia, 15 August 2022, https://www.worldhistory.org/article/2022/cyrus-the-greats-conquests/.

Waters, Matt, and Simeon Netchev. "Cyrus the Great's Conquests." World History Encyclopedia, 15 August 2022, https://www.worldhistory.org/article/2022/cyrus-the-greats-conquests/.

Wijnsma, Uzume Z. "And in the fourth year Egypt rebelled..." The Chronology of and Sources for Egypt's Second Revolt (ca. 487–484 BC." Journal of Ancient History, vol. 7, no. 1, 2016, pp. 32-61. https://doi.org/10.1515/jah-2018-0023.

World History Edu. "Cambyses II of Persia: History, Reign, Accomplishments, & Legacy." World History Edu, 15 November 2022, https://www.worldhistoryedu.com/cambyses-ii-of-persia-history-reign-accomplishments-legacy/.

World History Encyclopedia. "Persia Timeline." World History Encyclopedia, 2021, https://www.worldhistory.org/timeline/Persia/.

World History Encyclopedia. "Xerxes I Timeline." World History Encyclopedia, 2021, https://www.worldhistory.org/timeline/Xerxes_I/.

Young, T. C., and A. D.H. Bivar. "Ancient Iran | History, Map, Cities, Religion, Art, Language, & Facts." Encyclopedia Britannica, 2022, https://www.britannica.com/place/ancient-Iran.

Young, Jr, T. C. The Cambridge Ancient History. vol. 4, Cambridge University Press, 1988, https://doi.org/10.1017/CHOL9780521228046.002.

Printed in Great Britain
by Amazon

23290262R00086